TAROT

Learn the Secrets of Reading Tarot Cards and
Discover Their True Meaning

(A Guide to Psychic Tarot Reading Real Tarot Card
and Simple Tarot Spreads)

John L Scarberry

Published By Darby Connor

John L Scarberry

All Rights Reserved

Tarot: Learn the Secrets of Reading Tarot Cards and Discover Their True Meaning (A Guide to Psychic Tarot Reading Real Tarot Card and Simple Tarot Spreads)

ISBN 978-1-77485-352-8

All rights reserved. No part of this guide may be reproduced in any form without permission in writing from the publisher except in the case of brief quotations embodied in critical articles or reviews.

Legal & Disclaimer

The information contained in this book is not designed to replace or take the place of any form of medicine or professional medical advice. The information in this book has been provided for educational and entertainment purposes only.

The information contained in this book has been compiled from sources deemed reliable, and it is accurate to the best of the Author's knowledge; however, the Author cannot guarantee its accuracy and validity and cannot be held liable for any errors or omissions. Changes are periodically made to this book. You must consult your doctor or get professional medical advice before using any of the suggested remedies, techniques, or information in this book.

Upon using the information contained in this book, you agree to hold harmless the Author from and against any damages, costs, and expenses, including any legal fees potentially resulting from the application of any of the information provided by this guide. This disclaimer applies to any damages or injury caused by the use and application, whether directly or indirectly, of any advice or information presented, whether for breach of contract, tort, negligence, personal injury, criminal intent, or under any other cause of action.

You agree to accept all risks of using the information presented inside this book. You need to consult a professional medical practitioner in order to ensure you are both able and healthy enough to participate in this program.

TABLE OF CONTENTS

INTRODUCTION 1

CHAPTER 1: GETTING INSIGHT INTO TAROT READING 3

CHAPTER 2: SUIT OF WANDS 6

CHAPTER 3: TAROT CARD DECKS FOR BEGINNERS 12

CHAPTER 4: TAROT SPELLS 27

CHAPTER 5: MAJOR ARCANA TAROT CARD THE MEANING AND INTERPRETATION 38

CHAPTER 6: THE MEANINGS OF TAROT CARD COMBINATIONS 54

CHAPTER 7: TAROT COMMON SPREADS.......................... 57

CHAPTER 8: WHAT TO ARRANGE THE CARDS FOR READING - THE VARIOUS STEPS TO READ THE CARDS IN THE CORRECT ORDER 69

CHAPTER 9: LEARNING MORE ABOUT THE MINOR ARCANA CARDS 81

CHAPTER 10: THE STORY OF THE TAROT'S SYMBOLISM THE TAROT'S ORIGIN: AN INVESTIGATION 94

CHAPTER 11: UNDERSTANDING THE MAJOR AND MINOR ARCANA 106

CHAPTER 12: THE WORLD 115

CHAPTER 13: OVERCOMING COMMON CHALLENGES YOU MAY FACE WHEN STARTING YOUR JOURNEY. 136

CHAPTER 14: SAMPLE READING 144

CHAPTER 15: FULL COMPLETION OF THE MINOR ARCANA 148

CHAPTER 16: SPREADS, OR HOW TO PLACE THE CARDS TO GIVE A MORE ACTUAL READING 155

CHAPTER 17: READ FOR YOURSELF AND OTHERS 161

CHAPTER 18: STEP-BY-STEP INSTRUCTIONS FOR THE MOST IMPORTANT READINGS 169

CHAPTER 19: PENTACLES 177

CONCLUSION 181

Introduction

Everyone is always seeking answers to questions about what they don't know, and broadening their perspectives. However, most importantly people are interested to understand what drives a person. They are interested in understanding the risks or joys that any person could be facing in the future or even in the present. We're keen to understand the future and are always trying to find a connection between our past and the present. We believe this will help us to understand our future and discover more about our professional and personal lives , as well as any obstacles that we may encounter. The easiest method of doing this is by doing Tarot reading. It is a traditional art that can help us visualize the future and the being of the person. Do you believe it was actually the game of cards?

It is an most comprehensive guide for you if you are just beginning your journey. It can also be used to refresh your knowledge if you're considering the idea of giving a Tarot reading. It gives you all the details is required in the event of offering anyone the opportunity to give a Tarot reading. After you have finished the book, you'll be able to comprehend and know more about yourself and others via Tarot readings.

The different chapters inform you about the various cards available as well as the cards you'll require based on the circumstance. There is a set instructions to be aware of every time you use Tarot cards. Tarot cards. The book gives you details on how to utilize these Tarot cards in addition. The various chapters will explain how different Tarot cards can be read and what they can mean. The book also includes an example reading that will assist you in understanding the process by which readings are conducted.

Chapter 1: Getting Insight Into Tarot Reading

Before we can discuss how to read tarot decks It is crucial to understand what reading tarot cards is and how it came to be first introduced.

What is the Tarot And How Did It Come into Being

The Tarot refers to the playing cards in a set. At first it was known as trionfi. Its name was later changed to tarock and then taroxchi. Its usage became more commonplace in the late fifteenth century across various regions of Europe to play cards, such as French Tarot and Italian Tarocchini.

Since the 18th century the present, tarot is utilized to divinate by mystics and occultists. Like the popular game cards, the tarot consists from four different suits. Each of the four suits is comprised of 14 pip cards number-coded from Ace to ten. It is also made up of 4 face cards: Jack queen, knight and the king. Additionally cards, the tarocchi is one trump card from the 21-card suit, and a card known as the "fool. The fool is used as the highest trump in certain games, and can be excluded in some games.

The first recorded cards were created between 1430 and 1450, in Bologna, Ferrara and Milan in Italy when the additional cards with allegorical illustrations and illustrations were added to the back of the deck that was originally four-suit. This new and unique set of cards was called triumph or trionfi.'

Etymology of The Tarot

It is believed that the French or English word "tarot" is taken from tarocchi that is from Italian origin, and doesn't have any specific etymological roots. The singular form of "tarocco," which translates to "blood orange in Italian. The use of the word spread throughout the world the word tarocchi became the term tarock German and Tarot in French. There are many theories to its origins, however none of them is connected to divination or occult practices. One theory suggests it's related to the "Taro River located in the northern region of Italy close to Parma since the game of tarot originated in that region. Certain sources suggest that Tarot is derived from "turuq," which has Arabic origin. It is the Arabic word for "ways.'

Now that you understand how the tarot came into existence and what it was initially used for, let's continue to talk about the main cards.

Chapter 2: Suit Of Wands

The wand suit represents people who are observant and well-informed. It's also a symbol of people who are kind and compassionate. The cards usually relate to career and employment problems. They also refer to the movement of our lives, such as blossoming new beginnings. The suit is connected to elements of fire, and those who wear it with this suit are well-organized intelligent, rational, businesslike and energetic.

The meanings of the cards are as follows.

Ace of Wands

Upright, the Ace of wands represents the power of creation, creativity as well as new beginnings and enormous potential. When reversed, the card can be used for someone who isn't motivated or is burdened and is slow in achieving goals.

Two Wands Wands

The two wands up represents the future, progress decision-making, discovery, and planning. In reverse this card represents the fear of the unknown as well as a lack of preparation.

Three of Wands

The three Wands represents those who experience anticipation, foresight and growth. In reverse, the card symbolizes one who is sluggish and lacks foresight, and is likely to face difficulties in their long-term as well as short-term goals.

Four Wands Wands

Upright The card with the four of Wands symbolizes happiness peace, harmony, home marriage and community. When reversed, the card can stand for the breakdown of communication and a change that could be not a good idea.

Five of Wands

The five the wands indicates an individual who is in contest with another or in a dispute. There could be tension, strife and conflict. In reverse, the card symbolizes those who want to come to an agreement to disagree, and keep conflict at bay. They're diverse.

Six of Wands

The six wands that are upright stand for someone who is seeking the public's attention, recognition, victory and growth. The person is confident. If reversed, the card symbolizes an individual who is self-centered and lacks confidence, and has a bad reputation. They'll experience a decline in their standing.

Seven of Wands

The 7 of Wands that are upright signifies someone who is facing an event or contest and has the ability to persevere. If reversed, the card indicates those who are likely to quit because they're overwhelmed. They could be also overprotective in relationships.

Eight of Wands

Upright, the eight the wands cards symbolizes rapid, action, quick movements, changes, and travel by air. In reverse, the wand symbolizes an inability to move, a delay and anger.

Nine of Wands

Nine of Wands up indicates someone who is courageous as well as perseverance and endurance however, they'll be put through an examination of faith. When reversed, the card is an individual who is constantly at risk, anxious or unsure, as well as anxious.

Ten of Wands

The Ten of Wands card indicates an individual who is under plenty of pressure, burdens and obligations. They're very demanding to work with and could have an accomplishment in the future. In reverse, the card represents someone looking to get away from responsibility as they've absorbed too much responsibility.

Page of Wands

The wands' pages that are upright symbolizes someone who is enthusiastic and would like to be an adventurer. They are always looking for and exploring. The reversed card stands for those who are pessimistic and lacks direction. They'll experience setbacks due to their concepts.

Knight of Wands

Upright the knight of wands represents one who is driven for energy, passion, action, adventure, and are indecisive. The reversed card stands for someone who is prone to delays. They're extremely hurried, dispersed, and annoyed.

Queen of Wands

The queen of wands, is one who is radiant, warm and exuberant. They're extremely determined. The reversed card symbolises an individual who is aggressive, brutal or demanding and is shrinking.

King of Wands

The King of Wands standing upright represents the person who is a natural leader, entrepreneur and an innovator. They're highly respectable. In reverse, the card represents those who are impulsive and impulsive. They are ruthless, reckless with high standards for the people who surround them.

Chapter 3: Tarot Card Decks for Beginners

Tarot cards aren't as appealing in comparison to playing a standard deck, which has seventy-eight cards to choose from anyone who is a beginner can pick the pack and start playing when they are familiar with the basics. The cards included in the tarot pack are divided into a variety of categories:

Adjust

Smaller and Main Arcanes

Pip Card

Court Documents

Once you have a grasp of the various features of each type of tarot card, it is merely a matter of mixing and combining information.

The most basic arrangement of the Tarot cards is the 22 main Arcanes as well as the 40 pip cards, as well as the sixteen court cards. The most effective way to begin to grasp the meaning of the cards is to put every one of the 22 principal Arcana around a circle beginning with the first card in the middle. After that, if you look through this map from a clock-wise perspective, you'll be able to trace the path the soul's journey throughout its lifetime.

Within the first circle then put in 40 pip cards. It starts by putting a pentacles suit. This is the first twelve-position map that shows that winter solstice. In the third position it is possible to take the pentacles suit and follow it with the sword suit, which indicates Spring Equinox. Then , place the suit of the wand in a 6-hour location, which signifies that it is the summer solstice. Then, it concludes by presenting a series of Cups beginning at the point of the nine and indicating the autumn Equinox. Similar to how that the tilt of the principal Arcana is a symbol of a cycle, that of the PIP map illustrates the movement that the Earth around the sun over the seasons.

In the final phase, between these two circles, equally divide the remaining 16 Court cards, beginning with one of the queens to another within the seeds that are in that of the circle to which they belong. These maps highlight different significant people and how we change through the years.

When performing this test it is essential to remember that the fact that one card is in the upper circle or lower circle is not more significant in comparison to the others. Every card, no matter if it's Major Arcana or Minor Arcana, has a unique place in a Tarot reading.

Each seed within smaller Arcane has a specific meaning that play a significant part in the understanding.

Cups: The cups are linked to the element water. Like water, it can flow effortlessly, but it could also be interrupted by the dam or boil and cause anger during storms, as and our emotions. When you read the cards that are placed in the cups, it's crucial to understand the process of one through ten a purely emotional manner.

Chopsticks: The chopsticks are affixed to the element of fire. The fire element is has a energy and motion It can be used to cause destruction and creation. Chopsticks are therefore the basis of action and change. While reading this dress, you'll be able to see the first steps towards the beginning of a new chapter as well as the beginning of our future, and also cards which tell us that we made a decision too quickly without thinking about the future.

Pentacles: Pentacles are connected to the earth element. The Earth is solid, stable and grounded. It is the place where we construct our homes, eat and sustain our bodies. The same way, these dresses concentrate on the body and senses. It doesn't matter if it's creating an atmosphere where you feel secure or secure in your finances or taking good care of yourself while building an entire family, it all is possible by reading the pentacles.

Swords: swords are linked to the element of air. It is impossible to live without air and can't breathe. But, air can make you breathless in an the blink of an eye. Like the air, which is sharp and powerful and savage, the sword too. This outfit is focused on intelligence. There was a saying the intellect is the better weapon than words. So be aware of the dangers this seed may carry when it comes to communicating with other people. It also focuses on the necessity of mental clarity and fresh ideas.

It also considers the people who are represented in court's records. These cards are crucial to read because they could be directly connected with you, or to someone else who closely relates to your particular situation. Sometimes, it helps us identify who we could seek help from or who might hinder our advancement.

Pages and princesses can be interchanged, and your deck is likely to have one or the other but not both. In drawing a princess you will read about someone who seems young. They may have unrealized potential that is not recognized or acknowledged, or arein reality actually a child. A princess could refer to an individual who is a student or has just begun the next chapter of her life.

Princes: Princes are often paired as Knights during a tarot card reading The bridge may include either one or the other but not both. The concepts represent the power of movement and action. They seek to make progress in their lives and are often optimistic. People who look like princes are cautioned about decisions without thought because they tend to take a leap of faith and believe that everything will be fine in the best possible way. Princes are thought to be enthusiastic about every aspect and are considered to be a kind of person who is willing to assist others.

Queens are regarded as compassionate and intelligent people. They are highly regarded and loved. They inspire rather than imposing. The Queen may represent women or men in the event that she exhibits the above qualities. Most often, they are either a mature individual or a person with a close relative who has experience to use in giving guidance.

Kings are a symbol of someone who was a child in his time and is now mature and perfect. Most often, the person depicted by this card feels the greatest obligation and responsibility toward others, and will put the needs of family and friends family over their own needs.

After looking at the categories of seeds, court cards and the best way to arrange a deck of tarot decks to understand its history the significance of each card will begin to be apparent. In this moment it is possible for a beginner to choose one of the deck cards and give at the very least a basic definition. When you are confident with this information take a look at the numbers between one and 10 and then examine all the mystery cards one at a time. Once you've a good understanding of the meaning behind each number and what the titles of the principal arcanes mean it is then possible to interpret tarot cards from Marseille. It takes practice, and at times, you might require a Table of Reference, but gradually and gradually, you will be able to comprehend the ideas that are behind the categories of tarot cards and anyone can learn and become a simple and basic Tarot reader.

Create your own Tarot Card Deck

It is a Tarot Card game one that a lot of people would like to try, but I'm not sure of the strategy to go with. The variety of games on the market can be quite a shock to certain. Even if you enjoy a couple of tarot card games, you might not have the money to buy several. Instead of perusing the various Tarot decks that are available now is the time to create your own tarot deck to your needs.

You'll need a few things prior to making a Tarot deck for yourself. In the beginning it is necessary to use a more dense quality paper, on which you can draw sketches of Tarot. If you come across a paper that has a pattern one side, and an empty area on the opposite the paper is more appealing. You can cut it into 78 equal rectangles or squares, according as you like. Gather artistic materials to draw on the side that is empty on the sheet. Things like markers or colored pencils are great because they aren't smudge-prone.

If you are looking to replicate the concepts of a traditional tarot pack You should search for a real Tarot deck or card on the internet. In this way, you'll begin with an idea to each of the cards, and you can design your individual designs. Take a look at the examples of tarot for an inspiration source; it doesn't have images that you have to replicate. You can, for instance, draw a five-stroke. However, the chopsticks are able to look however you'd like and there might be other backgrounds that you choose to are able to.

In order to complete the set it is necessary to make an area that is secure during times when it's not being used. You can purchase a box or bag that could be used for storing your cards, for instance. You can then decorate the box or bag to make the room more unique and distinctive. Many people choose the option of putting their card in a laminate for an extra layer of protection and security.

Whatever the reason you are seeking out a tarot card, keep in mind that you don't have to shell out on a large sum of money, or even stick to "traditional" designs. To anticipate the future, start by creating cards with your own hand.

How to foretell the future with Tarot Decks Tarot Deck

Is it possible to forecast the future? What do you think of using the Tarot deck? Yes, it's there! Check out the article, and learn the process.

Find your favourite tarot deck and fortune-teller. It is best to remain in a calm space, however, the main thing to do is work using cards. They are all wonderful tools that help to create a tranquil environment. It is best to use the tarot or Oracle decks. They can be used to ask open questions instead of yes/no questions. Some open question strategies are given below. The answer to a yes/no question is to cut off the petals of a daisy, "does she love me? Or don't you like me? "I am getting an increase."

What kind of energy do I be able to track in July?

My annual test is scheduled for the final week in March. What areas for improvement will be addressed in my exam?

I'm planning to propose to my girlfriend. What's the most appropriate date and week to propose to her?

My son is about to start an entirely new school. What do we need to learn about the school? What will the changes do to help him successful?

The next Monday is Saturday, so what motivation do I need to bring to work? House? In the middle of the highway?

Make sure you take your time, write down your questions and research each one. Be sure that the question you ask is the exact thing you'd like to learn. Inquiring questions that are not specific will yield an answer that is often unclear and frustrating. A good example of a question that is vague is: "why can't I find an ideal job? The alternative is to think, "What kind of energy will I need to acquire an even better job?"

After you have formulated and thought about your question in the context of the time you were seeking education, use to the Tarot platform (or Oracle platform). Mix the cards, and then think about your query. Get the maps. Take a few minutes to meditate with the map. Consider the story that the map tells you , or the story that causes you to think. The story could involve Little Red Riding Hood, or Uncle Ted found an area of wildflower. It doesn't matter what the history is either real or fictional. Take a look at the colors and see what they mean to you. Take a look at your numbers and the times as well as the symbols you find in the map. Remember the ancient traditions associated with Tarot meanings.

In meditation, concentrate on the map that is represented by the shape, symbol or color that symbolizes the shapes that the maps. Let the shape, symbol, or color dance through your mind until you can form the next. In your calendar, sketch it out or write it down along with any other details you have received. Don't judge the information you receive. Note down the information. The image of a vessel falling into Blood Red Sea may not be a true wreck. It could be a sign that on the 15th day of January of the year to come the business you work for might experience massive drops in the value of its shares, and be financial sluggish. Take note of every detail regardless of whether it's logical or it doesn't.

In what way is it required to ask for information in the near future. If you're looking for information about next week's events or seven months from now It doesn't matter. The custom is to not ask to know more than six months prior to the event due to the fact that the vibe about the event, person, etc. may alter. The same is true for any measurement. After two hours, the energy levels could shift for at least two decades in the near future.

If you've received forecast-based data You should think about reconnecting to maps at least a week or a month prior to that forecast day. People make changes to their mind or acquire new abilities, and even die, but they can also be anything which can alter the course of time. If something is changed or not is a clear answer. If the situation is completely different, it is possible to find out what new forces are affecting the day.

Be vigilant for cards, labels, symbols, colors, etc. that appear in all of your predictions. The more often something happens the more likely it becomes.

If you are reading about others take note of the pattern of repetition on the cards. If you spot any cards, they repeat and again, regardless of which person who is reading. This can happen for anywhere from between four and six months. Attention. If the tower's map is displayed at every reading, it could indicate another bank's collapse. If the moon appears, it may be a sign that we're taking an emotional reaction to the incident. In any case, whether the map or no map, this pattern of repetition indicates that something is changing. There is a change happening in society or politically. Or economically.

Predict your future now by pulling up your calendar, or dial the phone. Remove any tool that you can to live the normal routine. Utilizing tarot cards or Oracle decks it is possible to determine the future.

Chapter 4: Tarot Spells

Tarot spreads are the way that the tables are set up with the cards. There are numerous spreads for tarot, and the main difference is the method in which they are laid out.

The first spread that I want to examine is a simple spread of tarot and is known as"the Celtic cross. It is laid the first card on the table. Card two is placed on the top of card one, with the opposite side facing and is placed near the lower part of card one. It is placed right below card one. Card 4 is placed just to on the right side of card 1. 5 is placed over card one, and 6 is just to the right of card one.

You will now move to the right of card 6 Place card 7 on the table. 8, will be placed over 7 and 9 above 7, and 10, above 9.

This spread is generally used for general readings however it is also utilized for a specific question-based reading. You must be aware of how the positions of the cards impact the cards within this spread.

Within the Celtic spread:

Card 1 details what now affecting the person who is looking for answers.

Card 2 outlines the obstacles which are preventing the person in search of answers.

Card 3 is a description of something that has occurred in the recent past that has had a direct impact on the present scenario.

Card 4 describes past circumstances the seeker been confronted with.

Card 5 explains what the seeker hopes to accomplish.

Card 6 provides a description of what future prospects for the seeking have if they keep following the current path following.

Card 7 can be used to determine the attitudes of the individual seeking help with their current situation.

Card 8 describes how other people are able to see the seeker.

Card 9 can help the person looking for it to understand their fears and hopes.

Card 10 outlines the ultimate result of the situation, should the person continue to follow the same path they're currently following.

This time, I'd like to clarify that when I say that the person is still following the same path they're following, it's a sign that the fact that a tarot card reading indicates that something is likely to occur, it doesn't mean that these events are fixed in the ground. It is important to talk with the person about the different paths they can take to prevent negative outcomes from certain situations of their lives.

This is the one which most people use since it is a fundamental spread of tarot, and it's extremely easy to comprehend and also keep track of what the different cards' positions mean for each one.

The next step is to make the five-card spread. The first card you lay on the table. This will be used as the center for the spread. The other four cards will be placed around card one. The second card will go below the card one, the card 3, on the right of the card one, the fourth card will go beneath card 1, while the fifth card will lie over card one.

This is a very easy spread, but in order to use it, you need to understand the meaning behind each position.

The one card position in this spread is the present situation or space of life for the seeker within which all other cards are centered.

The second card in this spread is a representation of the influences from the past in the lives of the people who remain in effect on their lives. It typically represents something from the past of the person that is directly impacting the present situation, which is symbolized by the first card.

The position of the card three in this spread is the future for the seeker in the scenario illustrated by card one should the seeker continue on their current course.

The four-card positon of this spread signifies the reason that the person asking the specific question . It generally sheds some clarity on the meaning of the card two.

The position five in this spread is a representation of the possibilities that exist depending on the scenario. It doesn't provide a definitive outcome, or predict the future, but it can provide positive results in the event that the seeker makes a change to the direction they are on , or a negative result in the event that the seeker follows the same path , and the reverse.

This is a great spread for those who are seeking an exact direction in a particular area of their lives.

The following spread is the one with an ellipse. It contains seven cards designed in the shape of the shape of a V. The first card is at one of the highest points of the V, followed by 2 and 3. 4, which is the center of the V. Then follow five and six with seven ending the opposite part of the V.

The first card of this spread will explain how the past has been impacting the present situation.

The second card of this spread is intended to provide a description of what's happening in your personal life and can affect the circumstance the seeker wants answers for.

Card 3 of this spread is expected to explain what influences will be in play depending on the particular situation.

The fourth card of this spread will describe what the seeker must take in the present scenario.

Card 5 of this spread is expected to provide an explanation of any external influences which have an impact on the present situation.

The sixth card of this spread will be discussing the fears and hopes of the seekers.

Card seven in this spread will address what the end result will be of the scenario if the seeker stays on the current course they are following.

The fourth spread I'd like to share with that you to master is called the relationships spread. This spread has 10 cards, laid out in this way:

One card is placed out on the table and followed by 2,3 4, and 5, making a row of them. Cards 6 and 7 are placed on top of card 3, card 7, is placed beneath the cards 3, 4 and 5. Card 8 will be placed under cards 2 and 4. The card 9 sits over card 6, with card 10 on the right side of card 9.

After you have the cards laid out, it is important to be aware of what the cards means.

The position of the card within this spread can reveal the distant past of relationships.

The position of the second card within this spread can provide the past events that have impacted the relationships between the seeker and the other cards.

Three positions on the cards within this spread is going to explain the current state of affairs.

Four card positions on this spread can outline what external forces affect the relationships between seekers.

Five cards on the card on this spread is going to define the attitude of the seeker towards relationships.

The position of the card sixes on this card will explain any energy that is beneficial and can be employed for the gambler.

Seventh card position within this spread is going to be the basis for the future influence.

The position of the card eights on this spread be discussed any obstacles that the seeker may need to over come.

The card nines position during this spread is going to talk about the fears and hopes of the seeker.

The card tens position within this spread is going to be discussed the ultimate outcome should the seeker continue in the direction they're following.

The final spread I'm hoping to show to you is The mirror spread. The spread is made up of eight cards, and is laid out in the following manner:

Card one is laid on high on top. The remainder of the cards are laid down below the card to either the right or left of card. Card two will be placed to the left and below from card one. Card three will be beneath but to the left of card number one. Card four will be below card two Card five will be below card number three, card six will be below card seven and card six will be under card 5. The last card, card 8, will fall to the lower end of the spread, exactly in parallel to card one.

Once you have a better understanding of how to layout this spread , you can begin studying how the placements of each card impact their significance.

The first position of the card in this spread symbolizes the seeker.

The second position of the card in this spread indicates how the person seeking the card who sees others in the scene.

The position of the three card in this spread represents what other players in the scene are to the person seeking it.

The fourth position card in this spread symbolizes the challenges within the scene.

The position of the five card in this spread reflects what other people in the scene see themselves.

The six-card position in this spread defines your character to other players in the scenario.

The position seven in this spread is a description of the strengths of the situation.

The eight position of the card in this spread focuses on what will happen should the seeker continue to take the same route they're following.

There are many different spreads you can choose to use using tarot cards. Some focus on specific subjects like love or careers, while others generally-oriented spreads. The ones you've learnt in the chapter you've just read are the basic spreads that you can use in the beginning of learning about tarot decks all the way through to an expert and above.

I would suggest starting by learning the Celtic cross. Once this spread is understood, it is possible to move onto an additional spread and study the other one. Be patient as you master spreads. If it helps you draw the spreads on an notebook. You can also write down notes on what the different cards represent.

Chapter 5: Major Arcana Tarot Card The Meaning and Interpretation

There are two methods to master the art of reading Tarot cards. The first is to learn and remember the most common symbols that are used in the tarot , and also understand the meanings of every one of the Major Arcana cards. In addition, you must discover how to tap to your innermost feelings and be open to your intuition. You must connect to your own inner self that connects you to the universe. This is the basic structure of tarot reading.

There are 22 Major and fifty-six Minor Arcana cards, spread across four suits which include Cups, Pentacles the Swords, and the Wands. These Major Arcana cards, also called "trump cards," form the foundation of the whole Tarot deck, while those of the Minor Arcana cards deal with the diverse aspects of your daily life. There are many types of decks available in the market. It is important to select one that you can to establish a relationship with. If you can feel the deck, you should be able to touch different decks , and then hold them. Select ones that give you sensations of strength inside. If you're not able to hold them, look at the images of the decks and pick one that captivates or excites you.

Let's begin our journey by understanding what are the Major Arcana cards and deciphering the meanings of all the cards.

What are the major Arcana Cards?

THE MAGICIAN

The Major Arcana cards are the foundation for the Tarot deck. It is comprised of 22 cards, of which 21 cards are numbered . The other one card is not numbered, and is known as the "Fool'. Each card represents the way to spirituality, self-awareness, and self-efficacy and symbolize the various stages that we experience throughout our lives as we seek greater understanding of ourselves and our lives. They hold inside them a wealth of knowledge and lessons.

They also depict the basic nature of human consciousness , and teach the lessons that have been handed from generation to generation. The imagery of these cards is enhanced by wisdom and shrewdness from many different esoteric cultures and traditions from diverse religions like Hindu, Hebrew, Sufi, Buddhism, and Christianity. These cards are 22 Major Arcana Cards are known as Mandalas of the Tarot. Mandalas are elaborate designs that are painted on the canvas. They are utilized for meditation and as spiritual studies guides for the Tibetans. It is therefore essential to look at the images of these cards in order to understand the message they intend to convey. To do this, you have to connect deeply with your intuitive part and attempt to discover the message that the card is trying send you. It is important to look into your own personal meaning for the cards in order to understand the message.

Role Of Major Arcana Cards In A Reading

If you're Tarot reading is mostly comprised of Major Arcana cards, then you'll be focusing solely on the life-altering situations that you or your client are experiencing. These experiences have a greater effect on your daily life. They provide you with important lessons that you need to devote your attention to if desire to progress in your spiritual and personal journey.

The most important thing you must be aware of when conducting the tarot reading is to pay full concentration on the card. If you or the person you are reading for are not paying attention, a majority people who read Major Arcana cards that are part of the spread are likely to reversed. This could be due to not paying attentively to the reading and the lessons that are being imparted by the cards. Moreover, you must reread the meaning that was presented in the earlier spread prior to going towards the next. It is possible to conduct an tarot card reading using just these 22 important cards. It will give you insights into your spirituality as well as your thoughts.

The Meanings of The 22 Cards

Let's take a take a look at the names and meanings of these cards. Major Arcana Tarot cards. The card's number is displayed over the image of each card.

The Fool

If it's upright it represents fresh beginnings, spontaneity the spirit of freedom and innocence. If it's reversed it is a symbol of naivety, foolishness as well as recklessness, risk-taking and naivety.

The Magician

THE HIGH PRIESTESS

When it is upright, it indicates strength, skill, focus, and being efficient. If reversed, it indicates lack of planning, manipulation and hidden abilities.

High Priestess High

If it is upright it is a sign of the mystery of high power of the subconscious mind, intuitiveness. If it's reversed it reveals hidden motives and the necessity to listen the inner voices of your mind.

The Empress

If it is upright, it indicates beauty abundant, nature feminine, fertility, and femininity. But, in the reverse situation, it indicates dependence on others and blockage to creativity.

The Emperor

In the upright state the Emperor represents authority and structure, father figure , and solid base. If it's reversed this indicates dominance, control rigidity, rigidity and inflexibility.

The Hierophant

If it is held upright the card represents the group's identity, tradition the beliefs you hold, the adherence to a religion, and conformity. If it is reversed, it signifies going against the status quo as well as restrictions.

The Lovers

THE LOVERS

When held upright this card signifies love, relationships alignment, unity choice, values and choices. If reversed, it represents conflict, disarray, or misalignment in the values, and imbalance.

The Chariot

If upright, it symbolizes the power of will, assertion control, determination and triumph. When it is reversed, it indicates an aggressive attitude, as well as an absence of direction and control.

The Strength

When it is in an upright position it symbolizes confidence, control, patience and strength. If it is reversed, it indicates vulnerability, inability to control oneself and self-doubt.

The Hermit

If it is upright If it is upright, the Hermit represents inner guidance, solitude and soul-searching. If reversed, it symbolizes solitude, isolation and withdraw.

Wheel of Fortune Wheel of Fortune

If you are standing upright the symbolism is the cycle of life or a turning point in your life destiny, karma, and good fortune. But if it's reversed, it is a sign of external power that is negative, and can be uncontrollable or bad luck.

The Justice

If it's upright, it's truth fairness, fairness and causes and consequences, as well as justice. If reversed, it indicates the lack of accountability, bias and dishonesty.

The Man with the Hanged Man

If it is upright, it signifies sacrifice, the letting go of things, restrictions and suspension. If reversed, it signifies the delay of things, uncertainty, and martyrdom.

Death

If it is upright, it represents the beginning and end of a cycle, as well as change as well as transformation. When it is reversed, it indicates the inability to progress and a resistance to changes.

The Temper

When it is upright, it displays the balance, purpose to be patient, as well as moderateness. When it is reversed, it reveals excess, imbalance, as well as the inability to look at things over the long term.

The Devil

If upright, it translates to materialism, sexuality, addiction and bonds. If reversed, it signifies the power that was reclaimed by breaking free and the separation.

The Tower

If upright, it signifies the sudden occurrence of revelation, upheaval, change, or even a catastrophe. If reversed, it refers to the fear of change and avoiding a catastrophe.

The Star

When it is in a straight position it represents serenity in the upright position, inspiration, renewal faith and the possibility of hope. When it is reversed the symbolism is desperation, insecurity and lack of faithand also discouragement.

The Moon

If it is upright, this card symbolizes anxiety, insecurity, illusion, and fear. If reversed, it indicates discontent, release of anxiety and confusion.

The Sun

If the deck is in the upright position, then it signifies optimism and success, as well as vitality, joy, and warmth. When it is reversed, it represents the failure of the person and temporary depression.

The Judgment

When it is upright, it symbolizes the inner call, rebirth and judgement. When it's reversed, it's a symbol of self-doubt and a refusal to look at your own self-worth.

The World

If it is held upright the card represents achievement and integration, the completion of tasks and travel. When reversed, it symbolizes the lack of closure, and being unable to finish the task at hand.

This is the complete set of cards from the 22 Major Arcana card decks. It is evident the upright and reversed side of the cards can have different meanings. This is due to the fact that one card may mean different things depending on the person who is reading it. It is all about the sensation that you experience when you touch and taking a look at the card. Let's discuss how to disperse the cards and understand the meaning of them.

Chapter 6: The Meanings of Tarot Card Combinations

Let's take a look at some possible combinations that could be significant to you with regards to your relationships and overall achievement in your life.

The Magician as well as The Chariot

If these kinds of combinations are present in your reading, it is a sign that you will achieve what you want. This is because you've got confidence and courage to change your situation to your favor.

The Fool plus the Star

These numbers tell you that it's time to take the risk and venture into new areas particularly in your company. There is a good chance that circumstances will improve.

Power and the Emperor

This means that there's an uncertain future for you. There are likely issues with the authorities. You should be prepared for it.

The strength and the Ace of Wands

There are likely to be difficulties in the new position. Your business may experience losses. All you have to do is persevere, and everything will be in order at the end of the day.

The Hermit and the Hanged Man

This means that you're not happy, particularly in your relationship. This is due to the fact that you're waiting for the perfect partner that will never arrive. Thus, you should take advantage of the best life has to offer you, and let go of your "perfect" relationship.

The World plus The Devil

This combination of cards indicates that you're about to be free from your negative habits. It's a sign of ending your weaknesses or addiction to medication, feelings of helplessness, alcoholism and so on.

Strength plus 3 Pentacles

This could mean that you are experiencing an issue in your business. It is possible that you are facing difficulties in your work or even the projects you're involved in may not have a future. If that occurs, then change your career, job or even your business.

The Magician plus King of Cups

This is a sign that there's a deceitful person who is manipulating your. This is the reason your activities are heading to the opposite direction. Be aware and investigate on the those around you.

The number of possible combinations which could be seen that we can't cover them everything the possibilities in this article. But, this is the first of the many things you'll must learn about Tarot reading. Don't stop there. Be a better learner and master since this is the only way to become more proficient in tarot reading.

Chapter 7: Tarot Common Spreads

There are a variety of spreads that can be used to read tarot cards. Of these, spreads, the Celtic cross spread as well as the Yin and Yang spread are the most well-known. Three Card Spread Three Card Spread is the most simple and basic of the various kinds of spreads.

Three Card Spread Three Card Spread

A three card spread can be the simplest spread to use for Tarot reading. This is the ideal spread to gain insight in the present, past, and the future. While the Tarot isn't able to forecast what the future holds, it does provide some insight into how you feel towards a specific date. It is an excellent option to master the three card spread prior to diving into the two other spreads discussed within this section.

You'll need to divide the three cards drawn in the manner below.

The center card will reveal your personal story and how you feel at this particular moment. The left-hand side provides information about the many chances and obstacles that may occur to you. The final card, to the right, can help you find a solution for your issue.

Celtic cross Spread

The Celtic cross is one of the most well-known patterns employed during Tarot reading. It is a simple layout however, it holds a lot of energy. There is a lot of force behind this layout. This is because it has been employed by a variety of sects over the past couple of years.

Staff Cross/Circle

It is believed that the Celtic Cross is split into two pieces: the circle or cross, which is where six cards are placed and the staff, where four cards are set. This Cross / Circle is a model from the Celtic cross, which is located in Ireland. This cross features an arc that connects the spokes that are parallel to one another. It symbolizes the link to the spiritual realm and nature of all creatures and the events that occur in the present. The energies of the circular area are feminine and is in harmony with the energies from the staff area which is masculine.

The two sides in the Celtic cross are mirror images of the dual nature of nature. They show the polarities in the human mind.

It is a circle. Circle / Cross has two crosses. The smaller one that is located situated in the middle and consists of two cards, which is contained in the larger cross made up from six pieces. The smaller cross shows the specific event that is closely associated with your life at the moment of reading. The larger cross illustrates how events been happening from your past to your future . The card on the left of the cross depicts your past, while your card on the left of the cross shows the future. The cards on high on the crosses show your conscious mind, while the cards on the lower part of the cross represent the unconscious. The cards of the Staff section are about your past and don't deal with the current moment. To understand the meaning of the symbols in the Celtic cross spread, you need to allow yourself to follow the guidance of your subconscious. You'll be able to know your future more clearly and assist others in understanding their own futures better.

How do you interpret the significance of the positions within the spread

There are ten positions within the spread. This section explains how to interpret the significance of the cards based on these positions.

Position 1

The first place is the middle of the Circle / Cross. This is the position where the card is located on the lower part of the circle. The card in this position assists you in identifying the issue in front of you. The card also represents your anxieties and anxieties. It helps you determine the way you're handling the present situation. It helps you comprehend the way in which the situation affects your personal life.

Position 2

The second is the one in the middle of the Circle / Cross. The card in this position assists you in identifying the causes that cause the issue. It also assists you in determining the consequences of the issue that you are facing.

3rd Position

This card is located just below the middle of the Cross/ Circle. This card will help you find the root of the problem. It attempts to understand the issue and consider the bigger view.

Position 4

This position is located to just to the left of the Circle / Cross. The card attempts to determine what kind of incident from your past which is creating your current issue. It also assists you in identifying those experiences that you may be forced to let go to move forward in your life.

Position 5

This is the position at the center of your body. The card will inform you of your life goals. It helps you determine your moral values and your judgments. It can also help you determine whether there are any adjustments that you must change your behavior in order to create to a more positive future.

Position 6

The position of this card is just to the right of the middle of the Circle / Cross. The card will tell that you will be able to anticipate in the near future. It reveals the influence someone or something else could influence you. The card also reveals what kind of attitude you need to take to ensure a positive future.

Position 7

This is the lowest position on the Staff. It reveals everything about yourself! It will reveal aspects concerning yourself you may have never thought of prior to. It will tell you everything you must know about yourself and your appearance, viewpoint and how you conduct yourself. It informs you about your self - confidence as well!

Position 8

This is the second lower down on the Staff. The card you are in gives you information about the world around you. It will tell you how other people consider you in relation to them.

Position 9

This position is second from the top of the section for staff in the Celtic cross. The card in this position shows you the characteristics of yourself you must alter. It could also suggest that you modify your thinking to comprehend the issue better. It will help you recognize your fears and hopes.

Position 10

This is the most important position of the line of the Celtic cross. It offers an answer to your problem and provides the results of this solution. It also explains what you'll think of the solution , and the consequences either good or negative you could face as a result of the solution.

Yin Yang spread

This Yin and Yang spread throws the spotlight on situations in which the parties involved are in conflict with one with respect to one another. It is also a good option in situations where a person is experiencing feelings of conflict over a particular aspect of life. The two people may not be at odds, however they do disagree about a variety of issues. Sometimes, they have to seek out other solution to their issues. It is believed that the Yin Yang concept is founded upon its Chinese symbols of Yin along with the Yang circular shape that is made up of two symbols: one black and the second white, which is separated by an axis.

The opposing side

The cards in this set represent opposite aspects of the problem. Cards on the left (3 5 - 7 9) represent the side A. While they to the right (4 6 - 8 10) represent the side B. When you use this spread during the tarot reading, you put the cards in a different order, that is, you place two cards on each side side and one to the right. Repeat this process until you've placed the eight cards. Make sure to select the two groups, which are Side A as well as Side B.

The line of division defines the line at which opposite sides meet. The two cards represent the issue itself and the main problem. The main cause of the conflict is the one held by Card 11 which is the lowest card on the line of division. Card 12 is the one that Card 12 projects the outcome as the topmost card in the line of division. The cards that are in the middle of the line that divides are the ones with numbers 1 and 2. The following section explains how important it is to consider the position on the cards' spread.

How do you interpret the significance of the positions within the spread

The positions are similar to positions used in the Celtic cross spread.

Card 1 and 2/ Position 1 and 2

These cards reveal the root cause of the issue. The cards also reveal the impact of external influences on the issue at the time of issue.

Position 3 of Card 3.

This card will tell you the role of Side A within the equation. It also reveals the perspective that Side B holds the same position as Side A.

Position 4 on Card 4.

This card explains the role of Side B within the issue. It also reveals the perspective that Side A holds the same position as Side B.

Position 5 on Card 5

It explains the outcome Side A is hoping to get.

Cards 6 and 6 Positions

It informs you of the result Side B would like to get.

Card 7 Position 7

This card reveals the unconscious understanding of the issue for Side A.

Card 8 Position 8

This card shows the unconscious understanding of the problem, on behalf of Side B.

Card 9 /Position 9

This card gives direction to Side A on the best way to handle the challenge or issue at hand.

Ten Position Card / 10 Position

This card gives direction to Side B on the best way to handle the situation in present.

Cards 11 and 11 Positions

This card offers guidelines to both sides on how to resolve the dispute.

Card 12 /Position 12

The card you are holding will provide you with the solution to your problem.

Chapter 8: What to arrange the Cards for Reading - The various steps to read the cards in the Correct Order

Tarot cards work by placing them in a particular "spread". There are various types of spreads that you can work on for various situations, and reveal various kinds of information and amounts. Tarot spreads can be difficult and some may be extremely difficult to comprehend. We will therefore focus

The simple arrangement of just three cards, you can gain a better understanding of the way Tarot is used!

How do I get started?

If you're new to Tarot the three card spread is an excellent place to begin learning and practicing by studying Tarot cards! Even if your experience is a master reader the spread is perfect for quick solutions and getting back to basics.

The three card spread can be used to suggest an idea of a linear path as well as a sequence. The three-card spread could be used to solve a variety of situations and issues. To help you with this article, we'll focus on three cards which provide details about your present, past and the future.

Take your tools and materials

Tarot

Tarot interpreter book, or booklet

Optional: sage, candles, incense, etc.

Step 1: Choose a tarot deck

In the beginning, you'll need to buy a tarot deck! There are many decks on the market, and it is important to choose the deck that truly resonates with you. Select a deck you like visually. If you're novice to Tarot and are just beginning to learn about it, it could be beneficial to select something that has been widely used. The Rider-Waite deck of tarot is a well-known and popular Tarot deck that is a great beginning point.

Step 2: Locate an area that is quiet and private.

You'll need space and a peaceful environment to read in. Select a space that you are comfortable in and feels good in your body! It could be a place like your living room, bedroom or outside, for instance. Make sure to pick the right spot for you to relax and allows you to concentrate without interruption.

Tips: You can also add sage, frankincense crystals, stones or candles.

It's not required however it's a great option to set the mood and tidy up the space.

Step 3: Pay attention to an idea or question.

Before beginning reading, it is necessary to decide on a question or goal you want to achieve. Tarot cards can be a powerful instrument to help us comprehend the areas of uncertainty we face in our lives by revealing different perspectives through our subconscious. Thus, you should choose the topic that you are not in any way sceptical about. Questions must be clear and broad. Be focused on your question while you play with the cards, particularly when you are shuffle them.

Tips For those who are having difficulty selecting a topic consider your own questions about what it is you'd prefer to gain through studying. It could be as straightforward as "What do I have to look forward to in the coming month?"

Step 4: Shuffle your deck

Moving the cards around may appear easy, but it can be a challenge at times. Tarot cards are a lot bigger than normal playing cards and therefore you should be careful not to fold them. There are a variety of ways to shake your deck therefore it is up to you to decide which one you like. Here are some suggestions:

Make cuts in the deck. Slice the deck into various piles. Then, join them

Shuffle Method: Spread all the cards across an area of the floor or table before shuffle the cards.

Method of entry: Hold one half of the deck with each palm. Then, you can insert one portion of the deck into the opposite half at random.

Tips: Rememberthat there aren't "right" and "wrong" methods of mix the cards. Select the method of blending which is the most comfortable for you.

Pay attention to your goal or question while you play the game.

Step 5 Step 5: Divide the deck in three piles equal

Then, split the deck you shuffled into three piles. Place these piles next to each one.

Step 6 Step 6: Flip your cards

Flip the top card of every miniature stack, from right to left.

Step 7: Examine your cards

Before we interpret the reading, we must first be aware of what each symbol represents. There are three cards that are included in the reading.

Card 1: The past

Events from the past that have an impact on your

Events from the past that keep you behind or may be able to assist you

Card 2: The present

Your present situation

The challenges of the present

Card 3: The future of card

The scenario or the pathways that you could take in the endless possibilities

The result of the current scenario

Tips: Rememberthat the tarot reading you receive is the specific issue, topic or situation you'd like more clarity on. So, your cards can represent your past, current, and the future of your query.

Step 8: Create an idea of the cards you want to use

Make sure you are comfortable with cards! Take a look at the images on your cards. What reaction do you get to them? Do they leave you with any kind of impression? Do you have a personal connection to one or more of them? What are the colours or symbols appeal to you?

Step 9: Interpret your cards

It's time arrived to read your reading. Tarot reading can be challenging and requires a lot of practice to become proficient at. If you're a novice then you'll need an aid to explain what the meaning of the cards. A majority of decks with tarot come with an interpretation book for tarot or booklet. Additionally, you can use a variety of websites to increase your knowledge. Take a look at The Major or Minor Arcana and research the various aspects of their development, you'll see that you can get lots of knowledge on it!

Explore the meanings of the meanings of each card you have revealed. Consider how these meanings are related to your current, past and future in relation to the topic you are asking.

Tips: It is crucial to keep in mind that cards usually are used in conjunction. The overall image is more important than any one card. What is the relationship of the cards to one another? Are there patterns you can identify?

In general it is the case that generally speaking, the Minor Arcana tend to indicate the people, events and the issues that are part of our everyday life. They also represent the major issues that we face. Major Arcana, on the other hand, represent the larger themes that are part of our lives. They also refer to the larger themes of our lives. Major Arcana also refer to the general energies we deal with.

Be aware that reading the tarot spread is lots of practice! Although interpreting single cards is as simple as making sense of words, understanding a spread of cards is like speaking in sentences.

Step 10: Write down your reading

Also, keep a notepad and note the date, the question, and impression you have of your reading. This will allow you to track your progress, evaluate your performance (to ensure that you are making the correct interpretation) as well as keep the record of all you've learned.

Set up seven cards to create an open horseshoe.

When you begin to develop your tarot-reading skills it is possible that you have a preference for certain methods over other methods. The most well-known spreads currently used are that of the Seven Card Horseshoe spread. Though it employs seven distinct cards however, it's a relatively simple spread. Each card is set up in a manner that is related to various aspects of the issue or specific situation.

In this version of the newly released Seven Card Horseshoe, in order, the cards symbolize the past, present as well as the hidden influences of the Querent, the opinions of others, the way the Querent can do to deal with the situation, and the probable result.

The dispersion of the staff

Utilize the five-card pent spread to gain a better understanding.

The pentagram is a star with five points revered by numerous pagans and Wiccans In this symbol of magic, you'll discover a variety of significances. Imagine the concept of a star. It is light source shining in the darkness. It's something that's physically away from us, yet we all wanted to see that star in the night sky? It is enchanting. In the Staff, every one of five points have an significance. They represent the four classic elements that are Earth, Air, Fire and Water and the Spirit which is sometimes called"the fifth element. Each of these elements is included in this Tarot card design.

It was the spread of Romans

The distribution of Roma Tarot is simple, however, it offers a surprising amount of details. This is a fantastic spread to consider when you're trying to get a broad view of a particular situation, or if you are dealing with multiple interrelated issues which you're trying to resolve. It's a relatively simple spread that gives plenty of flexibility in the interpretations you make.

Many interpret that spread by the Romans as a simplistic assessment of the present, past and the future, using cards in each of three rows. The row below of row C contains seven more cards to illustrate the likely events within the life of the individual in the event that everything continues on the current route. It is simple to understand the Roman spread by taking a look at the present, past and the future. However, it is possible to get deeper and have greater comprehension of the scenario when you break it down into different elements.

The design that is used in the Celtic cross

Set your cards up as to create the shape of a Celtic cross.

The Tarot layout, also known in the Celtic Cross is one of the most intricate and detailed spreads that has ever been employed. It is helpful for situations where you have a specific issue that requires to be addressed, since it walks you in a step-by-step manner through the various aspects of the issue. In essence, it tackles each issue one at a and

at the end of your reading, at the last card, you'll have analyzed all of the various aspects of the issue in question.

Chapter 9: Learning More About the Minor Arcana Cards

The associations with the principal arcana card were discussed and discussed, it's time to dig into the meanings behind the minor arcana cards, also known as the ones that provide an insight into the things that happen in the life of an individual.

What is the Wand represent?

The suit, as it is connected to the Fire element represents changes. This element is believed to bring light and warmth; However, if it is not managed it could cause fire or even cause damage. Like the element, Wands symbolizes an individual's imagination and desire to make something. It also symbolizes the desire of a person to realize their goals. When this occurs in the reading of the client the message could be some aspect of their job or professional career or even their ambitions.

Similar to the major arcana, every card in minor arcana is associated with both negative and positive connections. For Wands the following could be explained:

Positive Negative

Engagement, determination, and passion Unpleasure, Reckless behavior

Although the suit may have general meaning, every card in it has its own meaning and can be found in the following table:

Positive Meaning of a Card Negative Significance

The Ace Creativity Process, Fertility Beginnings from scratch, Innovation Greed Insecurity, Frustration

Two Partnership, earned success Insane goals, Pride and

Three Convictions, New Ventures Partnership Frustration, Lack of courage, personality conflicts

Four Completion, New Home, Satisfaction Decadence, Impatience, Snobbishness

Five competitiveness, conflict Conflict, Acrimony losing because of devious tactics and fraud

Six Fulfillment, Great news, Victory Anxiety, Delayed news, Suspicion

7 Courage and Challenges Indecisiveness, Ultimate Success Timidity Loss of opportunities

Eight Action, Activity, Travel Delays, Impulsive action, Poor judgment

Nine Self-assurance, Inner strength Avoidable delays, obstinacy, Suspicion

Ten Over-commitment, Pressure Abuse the power source, Burden, Deceit

Page Enthusiastic, Hard-working, Loyal Impatient, Hyperactive, Spoiled

Knight Athletic, Unpredictable, aggressive, irrational and violent

Queen Independent, Practical, Warm Matriarchal, Overbearing, Vindictive

King Traditional, Fair, Courageous Intolerant, Autocratic, Prejudice

What are the Pentacles' meanings?

The pentacles are believed to be closely associated with that of the Earth element, represent stability and groundedness. It also has a connection with wealth material that can bring practicality and security. Thus, it is simple to understand that if the Pentacles appear in a reading, it relates to the person's financial situation and the potential it brings.

This suit may also have the following connections:

Positive Negative

Financial prudence, self-worth, stability, success Financial loss, greed, material obsession

The following relates to the positive and negative words that are associated with each of the cards that are in the suit

Positive Card Meaning Negative Significance

Accurate Recognition, Security Obsessions with Self and superficiality

Two different fortunes, foresight Journeys Distractions, impending troubles, inconsistent

3 Prosperity, Reward Teamwork bitterness, criticism and Delays

Four Contentment, material and emotional security. Material obsession, indecisiveness Greed

Five Financial loss, Hard times, Unemployment

Six Balance, Prosperity, Charity, Money management

Seven eventual success, perseverance Continuous effort, Failure to grasp opportunities, despair, issues caused by the person

Eighteenth Change in Fortune Dissatisfaction and lack of direction, wasted opportunities

Nine Achievement, Material success, Solitude Financial instability

Ten emotional security, family bonds, inheritance and Wealth Family restrictions financial problems

Page Careful/conscientious, Loyal, Honorable Greedy, Impatient, Lazy

Knight Hardworking, Practical, Truthful Arrogant, Complacent, Lazy

Queen Compassionate, down to earth, responsible with the finances, materialistic and suspicious

King Patient, Practical, Trustworthy Insensitive, Jealous, Materialistic

Which Cups symbolize?

The suit is related to Water. Similar to emotional states, Water also has the capacity to fill containers (figuratively and referring towards the heart). The emotions are the "element of our lives" and could be harmful or beneficial for people. It is therefore easy to conclude that the Cup closely represents the ability of a person to manage their emotions and feelings.

A few among the diverse positive as well as negative implications that are associated with this suit include the following:

Positive Negative

Compassion, Contentment, Creativity, Happiness, Love, Understanding Hate, Jealousy, Lust, Sadness

Like all other suits every deck in this suits has its own negative and positive associations as shown as follows:

Positive meaning of a card. Negative significance

Creative, Ace Contentment Hopefulness Barrenness, Despair Love lost

A Love Two, Partners Dissolution, Understanding Betrayal Separation

The Three Creativity Method, Fertility Sex and happiness without love

Four Familiarity, Re-evaluation Depression, Fatigue, Over-indulgence

Five Reassessment of Bad Luck Instability, Futility, Sense of loss, worry

Six happy moments, Harmony, The past is shaping the future , Inability to confront reality, Nostalgia

7 Aspirations: Choice Love Imagination Self-delusion

Eight Breaking of Ties Development Dissatisfaction and Change Insanity, unrealistic goals

Nine Emotional Stability, Joy Complacency, Kindliness, Finding the fault of others vanity

Ten Peace, Love, Commitment Unsocial behavior

Page Caring, Creating, Love Insecure, Scheming, Selfish

Knight Creative or Artistic Energetic, Passionate, Irresponsible, Faithless, and Immoral

The Queen of Affection, Artistic Intuitive Vain, Loyal, and Loyal

King Charming Good Mediator, and soul of the Party Untruthful, Self-centeredness and Refusal

What are the Swords refer to?

The last of the suit that are minor in arcane includes the Sword. The suit is connected to air, which is the element of Air and symbolizes an individual's ability to think. This is why it is frequently associated to stress and anxiety. This makes this suit difficult as the tarot reader has to be adept at communicating the significance of the cards used in this suit.

Typically, this suit can be interpreted as having one of two meanings:

Positive Negative

The ability to make a decision, Ethical principles, Justice Truth Animosity, Conflict Disharmony, Illness Unhappiness

To understand the meanings of each of the cards in this suit, please refer to the following table

Cards Positive and Negative Meanings Negative Significance

Achieve Mental clarity, Requirements change, victory Destruction Injustice, Misuse of power

Two Equilibrium, establishing the strength to be friends despite difficulties, Peaceful mind Deceit, Disharmony Tension

Three New Beginnings, A bitterness Discord, Heartache

Four Tranquility, Depression of Withdrawal Isolation, Exile

5 Acceptance Deception, malice Refusal

A warming breath, a brighter future, A journey facing issues, procrastination

Seven Diligence Confusion, Indecision

Eight Patience Depression. Getting small rewards from working hard, Limitation

Nine Misery, Isolation, Disappointment, Deception

Ten Unhappiness, Devastation, Continued Suffering

Page Truthful, Loyal, Intelligent Critical, Devious, Sarcastic

Knight Intelligent, Witty, Courageous Impulsive, Reckless

Queen Independent, Intelligent, Perceptive Insincere

King Authoritative and Rational Intelligent Bully, Impersonal

What do you think of the court cards?

The minor arcana is divided into pip (from Ace to ten of the same suits) as well as court cards (Page Knight, Page, Queen as well as King). The pip cards represent of a particular person's circumstance or influence that can be observed by the theme that is depicted on every card. But, court cards don't really "tell the story". What do they actually refer to?

The court cards define an individual who exhibits the characteristics they are credited with. Although the meanings of every court card for each category are different, the characteristics of the person who is described on the card are identical.

The following information will provide a reference as to who will be identified when one court cards are used during a reading:

Page - A male or female child

Knight - young man 35 or less

Queen is a woman of any age

King is a person who is over 35 years old

How can we avoid confusion from happening in reading tarot cards?

A possible issue that newbies confront when giving details is the fact the fact that there are a variety of cards, as well as the meanings of each. This is not surprising, considering that the tarot deck is comprised of 78 cards. There will be confusion in the event that there is just too many things to be kept in mind. The confusion will become more evident as they begin to learn the meanings behind every card in the arcana minor.

However, this could be avoided by focusing on a particular suit before trying to discover the specific and general meanings of the cards in a particular suit. Before you attempt to discover a new suit is suggested that the previously acquired knowledge is applied in an exercise reading in conjunction using the main arcana. For instance, if the significances of the Wands are first learned after the major arcana the suit is to be considered when reading the following one. This gradual development will not only allow the tarot reader to remember more of the information they've learned, but it can also aid in improving their abilities to give an explanation using only the major suit and the suit they've learned of the minor arcana. At some point, they'll become accustomed to providing an interpretation using all of the cards within their deck.

Chapter 10: The Story of The Tarot's Symbolism The Tarot's Origin: An Investigation

The beginning in the Symbolism in the Tarot as we've just stated, every card of the Tarot is a symbol of an image, a number as well as a thought. We've attempted to keep away from induction to the greatest extent possible during these explanations, and therefore we had previously looked at numbers as they're the best stable element and provide the most consistent results when they are mixed. Based on the solid premise that we've formulated that we are now in a position to consider the images with absolute certainty.

We believe that, because of this you've got an image of Tarot of Marseilles one of the most correct in its image one or the 22 cards drawn in the works of Oswald Wirth; Maybe--and this is vitally important--you have checked them twice. It is at this moment, to arrange the cards on your table and observe the back of the cards the figures depicted on them in distress wear gowns from the Renaissance period.1

But, is this set of cards from an old cause? It's not as. Check out your figures more attentively and you'll before long you will see Egyptian images, including the three-cross (No. 5) as well as the Ibis (No. 17)and the ibis (No. 17) Renaissance costumes. They immediately prove how seventeen (17)] Tarot that is found in Marseilles is the most accurate representation of the basic Egyptian Tarot, marginally changed to reflect the age of the outfits. Only the wanderers can make the original pack perfectly.

The findings of the those who have investigated the Tarot have verified this truth by providing the most convincing evidence. Additionally, the Tarots created by Chatto 2 Boiteau 3 or more from Merlin 4, 4 show that the past supports our assertion. Merlin conducted his research inductively, and also, was being the first to discover the very first Tarot that was from Marseilles inside the Italian Tarot at Venice, the father of some of the subsequent packs. He also believed that he found the source for the Venetian Tarot in the philosophical pack of Mantegna.

In any event He was unable to decide on the place of birth for this pack as the one Merlin believed to be its source for the Tarot is, contrary to what one might expect, a resurgence, which was created from one initiates. It is believed that the Ars Magna of Raymond Lully was also delivered in a similar manner and is drawn entirely directly from Tarot. We've included for reference the packs of Mantegna that is described during the swap as the cards from Balding similar to the packs of Italian Tarots that are the basis from which the vast majority of our own cards are derived.

Table 1 illustrates the connection between Tarot cards and the layout of Mantegna should be reversed and, contrary to what may be expected, Mantegna's cards. Mantegna that are drawn from the Tarot according to the way we've written about. This is where we explore the subtleties of various Tarot sets. In the event the case could, that the presence of Egyptian pictures in the supposed Italian Tarots does not convince those who are interested just a couple of sentences about the changing in Tarots in the East, and of Tarot within the East and in other countries of Europe in addition to Italy will completely illuminate him on the subject.

HINDU TAROTS

In spite of the statements made by Merlin in the Tarot, the Tarot is a summary of the logical data about the people of old. This is evident by Chatto his inquiries to Orientalists in this regard.

The truth is that the Indians are the only people to play a round of chess known as the Tchaturcmga that is evidently derived from the Tarot as well as the manner which the soldiers are arranged in four different arrangements: Elephants ponies, chariots, and chariots infantrymen. It is believed that the Muslims of India also have a set of cards, which is taken from old pictures of the Tarot such as Ghendgifu or Gungeifu and Ghendgifeh. This game is comprised of eight sets of 12 cards.

CHINESE TAROT

Untrained eyes may have difficulties in interpreting the Tarot in this manner However it's the Chinese have offered us an argument for our attestation. It is in their plan of the Tarot that is referred into by the tableau found on page 88. We have determined the correspondences of the minor , what's plus, the major arcana and four of Tetragrammaton's' over the table that is being referenced.

The illustration that depicts this Chinese pack is available inside Court de Gebelin {The World Primitif (Court de Gebelin Monde Primitif) as well as within the works of J. A. Vaillant. In relation to the other European Tarots, we have duplicates of nearly all, and that is why we mention the various releases we have been given the authority to offer advice.

THE FRENCH TART PACKS

This Tarot that is part of Etteila is not of any symbolic value; it's an awful mutilation of the original Tarot. The Tarot of Etteila is utilized to afflict the crystal-gazers. Its only interest is the awe-inspiring nature of its numbers. It could be purchased at a cost of 5 or 8 francs from the infamous dealers of Paris.

The Tarot of Watillaux, or pack of the Princess Tarot recreates the minor arcana with precision. It is worthy of consideration on this particular report. It is worth considering. Italian Tarot, that of Besancon and Marseilles are without doubt the finest we have. Particularly the lastone, which successfully recreates the primitive symbolic Tarot.

THE GERMAN TAROT

In addition to the Italian one, we can be referring to The German Tarot, in which the images of the minor arcana are amazing. The Cups are referred to through The Hearts, The Pentacles, The Bells, The Swords The Swords, The Leaves The Scepters, The Acorns, Be whatever it is true that this Tarot is not a good one.

The TAROT OF OSWALD WIRTH

It was crucial to have an Tarot pack where the imagery was firmly established. The work was proposed by Eliphas Levi who defined the principles upon which it was to be built on and was subsequently used in the hands of the late Mr. Oswald Wirth.

The sharp medium aided by the guidance from Stanislas de Gnaita, has designed the layout of the 22 major arcana. The drawings are a replica of those of the Tarot of Marseilles as well as the symbolic modifications suggested by the research of Eliphas Levi regarding this crucial issue. Thanks to the tenacity of M. Poirel, who contributed to the project by printing the structures, Ave now has a stunning archive of a representative in the Tarot of Oswald Wirth.

This is clever, since Ave has just begun for those who want to explore the Tarot in all its entirety, and to learn an understanding of the Tarot of Marseilles and the one is that of Oswald Wirth. Both will be used for our explanation of the significance of symbolic meaning for each of the cards. However prior to beginning the study of these images through a card, Ave must determine if there is a method to expressly define the symbolism that is part of the Tarot.

What are the best way to define the meaning of the TAROT In conclusion?

As of today, we have and fully clarified that the Tarot communicates with the old or mysterious science in every possible way. If Ave is at this point, she seeks to discover a solid motive for investigating the images that it spoke to! In the 22 arcana that are significant it is possible to put the Tarot to one side for a while, and take a vow to adhere to this ancient method of studying.

Only this can help us to accomplish our goals by not focusing on the clarity of the images but in guiding us to create them in a unique way and analyzing them against standardised and universal norms. This is why we will begin to work on a new character, while keeping the distance of as far as can reasonably be expected, making the mistakes that result from the desire to explain the symbols of the Tarot with no one else instead of looking for the solution at their source.

The initial stage of the hunt for these exact images prompts us to think about the thorny question of the point of origin of images itself. It is not possible to tackle the subject, much less decode this question without any other opinions; however, we can in this manner, refer to the views of a few journalists regarding the issue. Truth is a thing that has Solidarity as its basic and understanding of various conclusions. A certain point will become a crucial source of guidance to us.

Louis Claude de Saint-Martin, the obscure scholar, states within his work, The Tableau Naturel des Affinities that the basic letter set is composed of 16 signs. He gathered this information insofar as we are able to make a judgement, from natural revelation, paired with the education of a mysterious school, in which he was among the pupils. Lacour in his book about The Elohim as well as the Gods of Moses, has determined inductively the existence of an orderly letter and a further assemblage of sixteen symbols.

Another writer, Barrois, seeking after the demands of a truly unusual nature, also arrives at the conclusion of the appearance of 16 crude indicators within the System of Dactylology. However, the works from Court de Gebelin, or the entire work of Fabre d'Olivet are most intriguing in this regard. Through the work he titled Langue Hebraique Restituee The last mentioned learned Initiate established the existence of primitive hieroglyphic symbols from which the Hebrew letters were determined.

Each of these essayists, starting with completely different perspectives agree with their conclusions which provides a solid argument to the validity of their research. In any event, it is crucial to determine whether these simple symbols are the primary source of both Hebrew, Sanskrit, Chinese as well as Greek letters. The nature of the source is strongly correlated with the character of the result, and more importantly the subordinate letters will respond to our reasons.

It is the Hebrew letters set composed of 22 letters seems to be desirable for us, because of the correspondence between the amount of letters as well as our Arcana within our Tarot.

In the next step, we'll be presented with, as the first part of our investigation as the Hebrew letters in the order of 22 letters. These letters are inferred from the hieroglyphics that contain 16 primitive symbols. The end of the story is not at the point that a bright light shines over us from all angles. William Postel 1 uncovers to us the link between Hebrew alphabet and Tarot; Van Helmont the Younger 2. L. C. de Saint-Martin 3 Fabre d'Olivet and 4 anger confirm our belief and finally, Eliphas Levi 6 throws the weight of his incredible knowledge into the investigation.

But, we'll be amazed to learn this Sepher Yetzirah, 1 an ancient book from the Kabalah is an examination of the development of Hebrew letters.

Chapter 11: Understanding The Major And Minor Arcana

Every Tarot perusing(reading) involves changing the arrangement of your Major or Minor Arcana cards, yet what is the difference? Tarot employs images and pictures that trigger emotions to aid in utilizing our instinctual abilities. Knowing the difference between Major Arcana and Minor Arcana is not difficult, but fortunately it's also easy to see.

The cards aren't designed solely to help you see the future but to help you comprehend your current perspective to help you shape those insights and change your routines to bring about the change you desire in your daily life.

A Tarot perusing will help determine whether we can gain from our experiences or if we're being overwhelmed by negativity and failing to look for that silver layer. Because we are living in a place by the importance of comparing to the rest of the globe and we all are experiencing similar experiences that provide us with a certain, unquestionable motivation to. Tarot readings aren't designed to scare our thoughts about the future, and that's why many people completely misunderstand how tolerant Tarot perusing is.

In the case of a divorce, for instance, when we end an abusive relationship, we're beginning an entirely new phase and are becoming more adept at identifying possible connections in light of the pain we felt.

First of all what can we do to gain an understanding of Major and Minor Arcanas? the form of a Tarot perusing suggestion for you to increase the intensity and depth of Tarot.

The Major Arcana in Tarot Reading

The Major Arcana is a development process we undergo when we encounter the challenges of life. The challenges we encounter allow us to grow and transform into a better version of ourselves. Tarot readings can assist us in using our experiences to grow by providing us with an 8,000-foot perspective of our thoughts and feelings as well as the patterns and consequences of our personal actions.

The cards of the Major Arcana help uncover our individual weaknesses that can bite our egos in the event we don't take the time to be honest from them. They may help us in understanding if we're on the wrong side of our self-esteem or giving fear an opportunity to outwit us. It is believed that the Major Arcana begins with the Fool card. The Fool is an amateur, who has to explore all 21 of the cards in the Major Arcana to get astute and provide assistance to others when they reach the card 22. which is the World that is a sign of the person who is adjusted to their capabilities.

Major Arcana: The Major Arcana encourages us tap into the most eminent parts of ourselves, such as the ability to think, creativity, instinct and power, the ferocity of our speech as well as our ability to decide the right thing to do when it's not to us, or the benefits of not having the time to think. Because Tarot readings are designed to give us the course of events, it is possible to learn about the ways we thought about the past that created our current situation and a forecast for the future to be.

The short version is that Major Arcana cards focus on extraordinary circumstances that form our beliefs at the core. They help us understand how we're shifting our goals or experience a change in our interactions. They help us move into higher levels of consciousness in which we are influenced by our intuition by recollecting our thinking patterns that are hindering or helping us, so that we can alter our larger goals and make better choices for our own greater greatness.

The Major Arcana reveals the times when we are taking advantage of our feminine energy and when we draw on our masculine energy. It makes us realize the strength of our feelings(which have always been present!) and allows us to direct our energy towards achieving worthwhile objectives. It can also help us discern towards the times when we rely heavily on logic instead of a more profound sense of direction which allows us to receive guidance from the spirit and be strengthened by the subtle messages of the realms of the soul as well as massive awareness.

There are amazing informational snippets of wisdom from each of the Major Arcana cards and they all have a fascinating vitality in the pictures and the concepts they address. Examine what each of these Major Arcana cards are attempting to do to learn more about the cards and begin to discover your own natural abilities.

The Minor Arcana in Tarot Reading

The smaller events and moments which lead to the major events of our lives are represented by your Minor Arcana in your Tarot browsing. These actions are influenced by beliefs and thoughts which can be beneficial or hindering. For example, the small display of eating the same McDonald's Upbeat Dinner consistently could be based on the assumption that we're eating to ease the pain we must manage.

The Minor Arcana cards provide us with our daily encounters that we encounter and aid us in understanding what parts of our brains are dominant under specific situations. The four divisions of the 56 cards in the Minor Arcana speak to our cash (pentacles) and our feelings (cups) as well as our thoughts and thoughts (swords) and our passions (wands).

Each of these four categories is numbered from 1 to 10. This makes it easy to use your Minor Arcana for uncovering the details of your mind's inner activities. The numbers that are even 4, 6, 8 and 10 represent the reassurance of life and events that happen according to plan. One is a new beginning while 10 represents the highest point of a small cycle in your life.

Each of the 4 suit of Minor Arcana are also accompanied by 4 court cards. These comprise the page, knight, sovereign and the Lord. The page indicates that you're a novice in a region, or just starting. The knight demonstrates that the quality of your region. The sovereign displays maternal traits like compassion and imagination, while the ruler shows more proportion of your grounded real-world side.

End

The Major Arcana cards are incredibly effective at helping you find the moments in your life that have shaped your character. They can also aid you in understanding the major patterns that guide your lifestyle and could mean the difference between getting married and not getting married, or having kids or not, or switching professions or not. Minor Arcana cards can help you identify when your thinking is off. Minor Arcana cards help you to recognize when your decision-making is based on fear, your thoughts are not working or when smaller victories are not far away. Both Major as well as the Minor Arcana are significant and flexible.

There are some who feel nervous when they view the cards, such as such as the Fiend, Demise or the Pinnacle and then go into an anxiety that something bad is going to happen. These cards aren't intended to create fear but are actually useful devices. The Fiend card is a sign of the possibility of a dependency regardless of whether it's towards an idea you have or a person that is negatively impacting you. Tarot reading is designed to allow you to perceive the world around you and your role in it in a more clear way so that you can protect yourself and make better decisions by gaining more information about your own. In addition, the pass card doesn't necessarily mean the death of a person, but the surrender of a piece of your self that you'll never will require as your soul grows.

For both, it's crucial to be aware that what's about to come isn't set in stone.

Some people are afraid of Tarot readings because they believe it reveals a future isn't theirs to manage. In reality, Tarot readings just uncover the patterns you can apply to create energy and allow you to make a decision when you're required to choose the right path or alter your course.

Chapter 12: The World

The World The World, a wonderful card we're always grateful for, shares an aspect and intention with the Death card one that[J Mills97] majority of us tend towards not seeing. It's similar to the death card that signifies closure. In any event it is a fact that death is something that happens. The World is something that we can accomplish. The World displays a great outcome of the event or project. This moment offers not just the usual positive benefits--pride satisfaction and recognition, but also something extra. This achievement is accompanied by an understanding of the connection between the beginning and the end, and an appreciation of the most positive possible development of the universe. In the present everything is in the right place. The World also shares a lot to all intents and purposes with the Fool as it signifies a new beginning.

The Universal Waite World is exceptionally impressive in its declaration of advancement, as it features a massive wreath of a shrub. The most significant thing that is evident in an opportunity for universal relationship which also appears as a four-fixed indicators of the zodiac that are found in the Wheel of Fortune, and the red stripes on the wreath of the sculpture reveals.

Core means:

Completely.

Legacy World Legacy World shows the completion of an adventure with an hourglass showing all the sand found in the bottom part. The zodiac signs surrounding the figure suggest the universal stream. The figure has shattered its veil, revealing it is also an experience of self-discovery.

The Shadowscapes card [J Mills99] shows the security of self-information. Her crown speaks to light Her belt is according to the craftsman, the proof of the truth. The concept for "as over, as beneath" is an additional part of universal stream. This figure has come to that conclusion. Her sparkling globe is a reflection of the moon.

The Minor Arcana

There are over twice the amount of Minor Arcana cards (if you add your court card(s)) than there are Major Arcana cards. This is due to the fact that the vast majority of our daily lives consist of everyday life events and not of significant events. These minutes may not be life-changing but as the majority of our lives however, they are important. It is possible to observe every single one of your joys as well as your disillusionments, fights as well as your accomplishments, joys and your family, friends and your loved ones in these images--the things and people that comprise your world.

Ace of Wands

As with the rest of the Aces as well, as with all aces, the Ace of Wands is a chance to win or a surprise. Aces show a moment in time , brimming with luck. The power of the aces is evident at times when conditions are favorable to take actions. Fast action is the efficient method to get the maximum amount of the leeway offered by the aces as the time doesn't last for long. If we don't grasp the favorable place of the chance the time will pass by. Aces are also seeds of amazing security. Anything that is planted or initiated at present is a possibility for growth.

Since [J Mills100] is a wands deck that is packed with the red hot energy of the many the wands. The energy is expressed in various ways: motivation, enthusiasm and mental fortitude, will be, action, and optimism. It is particularly suitable for work-related exercises as well as projects of all nature. Ace of Wands is the universe that provides us with an "approval" signal. It tells the player to "take charge of business"--follow with that thought or acknowledge the demand.

On the Universal Waite card, the image that shows the hands rising from the cloud reveals potential for a present being presented. The hand is alive, demonstrating the possibility of development as well as the potential outcomes within the offer. The cloud highlights the possibility of only a minute. If you stand for too long and the conditions could change.

Core means:

An opportunity to act.

The Legacy card the wand is floating over an area of earth and fire. Earth's normal component together with the energy of fire could produce amazing results. The wand is decorated with gemstones, demonstrating its transformational potential. The setting (or possibly rising) on the sun is a reference to the concept of this chance.

Two Wands Wands

The Two of Wands indicates balance between vitality and vision. To achieve something it is necessary to have the energy. The card indicates that it is time to collect or create this vitality. A lot of energy without bearing does not accomplish anything, however, to organize this vitality, we must have an idea. It's time to define expectations, and to be able to see the end goal clearly. From a variety of angles it is the time of imaginative visualization. Concentrating on the desired outcome is also a form of manifesting.

This Universal Waite card features the vitality of life and vision by showing it several times.

He holds his wand in place on the 3D square, which is decorated with red roses and white lilies depicting the virtues of the aim (vision) as well as passion (vitality) in separate.

Core means:

Creating vitality and enhancing your vision.

On the Legacy card red and purple-tipped wand to the left side demonstrates passion, while the slightly blue wand that is on the right is flawless. When we combine these in a way and combining them, we can find the best way to get the crate open and meet our desires. As it might be, currently, there we have two boxes. The creator of this deck suggests a different level of meaning, stating that the red wand represents materialism while the white wand is a symbol of spirituality. The balance between spirituality and materialism, at this point, determines the final form of the final result.

The Shadowscapes card has another feature of the wands on this card. The lion symbolizes courage. is required to harness the power created by the twin elements of vision and vitality.

Three of Wands

The concept of active waiting might seem to be contradictory in the way it is written; however, in reality it works like the act of actively tuning into. When you tune in dynamically the listeners are especially open to all the words spoken by the speaker and the way it's being spoken, as well as non-verbal communication and so on.

It is usually assumed to be passive; However, this isn't often the case. In football in football, an outfielder or a wide gatherer is the star in the field, but they don't sit there waiting for it to arrive. They're watching the action focused, ready and ready to take the ball. They have prepared the plan of what they'll do once they have the ball moving.

The Two of Wands, there is a strong emphasis on social occasions and discharging vitality towards a dream. It is believed that the Three of Wands is the time when the essentialness is let go and the final goal being established. It's a time with a strong belief in the outcome that is perfect and looking for it and doing whatever is necessary to help it become more powerful, and being ready to take action when it does appear.

Universal Waite card The figure is relying that the vessel will be in. It is believed by J Mills102 that it's certainly in the process of arriving therefore he's best to keep an eye for it.

The Universal Waite [J Mills104] card reveals the social aspect of the festival, which includes many people in attendance, and with additional on the road, as women raise their groups to give a welcoming manner. The wand-shaped brush and the wreath of flowers conveys the impression of a fleeting quality. It's a celebration, is not a continuous lifestyle. Enjoy yourself and be sure to welcome the event.

Core means:

Celebrate the conclusion in a series of actions or achievement of a plan.

The Legacy card demonstrates that these celebrations can connect everyone with a higher power such as the light beams that illuminate each wand. This provides a place to form within the wands. This energizing energy can be carried with us even after the party is completed, to help us during less enjoyable occasions. Recognizing that the celebration or holiday will be more than just a holiday, may make difficult times more bearable. But, in the end an image of a rainbow -- a sign of expectation is passing, allowing us to appreciate the temporary nature of the celebrations.

This Shadowscapes card is filled with vibrant springtime energy. The falling roses and the rose petals suggest a wedding, an exquisite celebration of a bond.

Five of Wands

The power of conflict can vary from rivalry which is typically viewed as positive, or even aggressive angry, usually thought of as negative. Conflict can occur in many different scenarios. It could occur during the course of a meeting for an advisory group, in the event of an emergency or even between family members or group members who are organizing a celebration or holiday. In the end, conflict involves people who find their desires or wills getting stifled by other's desires or wills. The individual's wishes aren't what another person wants Conflict is just an issue of this kind. However it is often a source of perilous destructive, angry, and damaging life force that's difficult to control and can hinder effective arrangements.

Its Universal Waite card shows many individuals , suggesting the situation as a group. All of them appear in a state of play and could be indicating than a contest, competition rather than a fight.

Core definition:

Conflict.

The Legacy card, there's only one character that is shown multiple times. Dragons are in plain sight. This card is not so much about gathering and more so about internal conflict--about the battle against one's inner dragons.

Shadowscapes is a card that gives one person a sense of calm. Shadowscapes card also provides an individual. It does not express the emotion of anger, or even negative emotions. Instead it focuses on the energy and excitement experienced when confronting and overcoming challenges.

Six of Wands

It's a joyful and open celebration to be perceived. The triumph or some other effect is portrayed. The person is the center area of focus and the centre of the spotlight.

Public praise is generally seen as positive occasions. The joy and satisfaction that comes from accomplishments or triumphs in and of themselves, but being admired by others surely adds to the happiness. Also, there is a sense of satisfaction felt by those who do the honoring, pride in the accomplishment of a partner, feeling grateful for the accomplishments and even a relaxing feeling in the presence of solid leadership.

The Universal Waite card shows people who are generally invisible. They set the stage but it's the person on horseback that's the main attraction. He is adorned with wreaths of laurel, symbols of reverence. People raise their wands in support of the saint. This card is believed to convey the idea that even though an individual is being praised everyone benefits in some way or other.

Core definition:

Recognition of accomplishment.

The Legacy card does not have the feeling of network, at least with regard to the other players. Instead, the social aspect is addressed by an arch that is raised to honor the legend. The story appears to be a grand and spectacular event, but despite being gorgeous and dramatic, it leaves an underlying sadness.

It is a card that comes from Shadowscapes also features a single person. He's clearly happy with his accomplishment, holding high his laurel wreath while sitting on an elephant, a lion and snail. There is a sense having everyone present--assuming that there is anyone available to take a bow in front of him.

Seven of Wands

Being in a position of protection indicates two things being in a position to protect as well as being a target. However, the "something to protect" is worthy of protection, or whether the attack really an actual attack or whether the result is favorable depends on the specific situation or the basis of reading different cards on the spread or on the specifics of the card in the deck that is being used. In any case being protected isn't a favored or pleasurable experience. It's common to be judged or abused or even pettyly treated. But, despite all that there are those who appreciate the opportunity to show their courage and determination now.

The universal Waite cards features an image of a man who is protected from the higher ground, which is usually considered to be a good location. The figure is, by all accounts, solid and stable. Even though he is dwarfed, it appears like [J Mills106] might win.

Core definition:

Defensiveness.

The Legacy card the figure is identified as [J Mills107] entering an entranceway. Various weapons, or enemies are in her path. The figure is faced with the necessity of defending her right to go on her preferred path. The bright light at the top point of her wand demonstrates that it is important to align with the things she believes as being correct.

The Shadowscapes card depicts the mother fox guarding her young from a deadly attack. The focus is on having something worth fighting for. This sense of direction provides the strength and determination to prevail. In this case, the fight creates a more emotional response. It's more raw, and more "life as well as the end of time" as opposed to the two other cards.

Eight of Wands

Every now and then, things happen quickly and this card is a reference to the minutes. At these times in our lives, we are not in control. It is possible that things are in perfect order, or at least we imagine, however, once they're set, they'll be affected by external influences. Additionally, we might assume that the plan will produce some sort of outcome, and[J Mills108] unpredictable outcomes may result. Eight of Wands quick action is the most important security, and it could agitate even the most carefully laid plans. It is a great way to facilitate everything. It can inspire us and help us find a different way fully.

The Universal Waite card shows events that are moving toward their final destination. The moment is on these events and their movements and our inability to exert any control over the situation.

Core definition:

Swift development.

The Legacy card offers a slightly different perspective.

The wands have been put in their place.

All appears to be together. The archer who has disappeared communicates with the star constellation Sagittarius and is accompanied by a surreal, quick energy. The manner in which this new vitality is likely to influence the current situation is not clear.

The Shadowscapes card is even more ambiguous. certainty. The unpredictable winds will carry those seeds for her mission wherever they'll go. And at the end of the day, there is more uncertainty...will they be buried in deep soil, or will they be able to find sufficient water and can daylight get to the ground?

If you choose this deck, there's no control and a far greater likelihood of being carried in an unimaginable method.

Nine of Wands

While this card isn't the most enjoyable of experiences but it is a representation of something extraordinary beautiful, beautiful, and exemplary. Today, take a look at the magic of wands. fire, in its most powerful form communicates the qualities of the human spirit. This is a sign that has been fought by fire and then improved because of it. Reliance quality, perseverance and vigilance are the most important qualities. Courage, vigilance and wisdom are the virtues that can be earned through hard work. A Nine of Wands indicates that the person who is being mentioned has had a difficult period, endured and become more grounded. The card also suggests that the person is anticipating and is ready for a new challenge. However, whether or not that actual challenge is stated.

On the Universal Waite card the figure injured is refocused. The main point of this card is the hushed-up patient readiness and complete autonomy.

Core definition:

Making preparations for the next challenge.

The Legacy card depicts a groundbreaking figure that is stooping under the light of the moon as well as the glow of wands that are near him. The edge of the wand that the man holds shines red, signalling the intensity and power of his intention. Yet, despite his physical power and strength of will, his act of humility shows [J Mills109] more quality.

In the Shadowscapes card, the warrior and his men sit and watch. Armed with determination Their injuries have were healed, but they weren't neglected, as they form the perfect image of strength and determination.

Ten of Wands

They are a part of a variety of types: duties, expectations of others, the necessities. They can be taken on either involuntarily or voluntarily.

It could be heavy throughout the day or are not even weighed at all. No matter how debilitating or a minor issue, whether it's permanent, infrequent or temporary, the card does not tell us whether we should put down the burden, discover an alternative method of carrying it, or carry on carrying it. It basically states the existence of it.

Universal Waite card shows a specific figure that is carrying an uninspiring load when walking towards an objective. The load makes the journey more difficult and not practical. The only conclusion here is that the goal of figuring out a feasible speed while carrying the wands be accomplished. It is not difficult to ask whether there might an alternative method of carrying the wands?

Core means:

A significant weight or a number of weights.

In on the Legacy Card, we can see an image of a man with a heavy weight that actually blocks his progression. It's not at all like those of the Universal Waite cards The card appears as if a choice must be taken.

The Shadowscapes card the weight seems to be more hefty and unfavorable as compared to other cards. The tree has an responsibility to do so the extent to which it is. The the world she carries on her back blocks light, symbolically depleting the vitality of her. Her future prosperity is at stake.

Chapter 13: Overcoming Common Challenges You May Face When Starting Your Journey.

Picking a deck

This is among the first concerns that new individuals ask themselves.

For Tarot cards, decks have a more significance because it's one that you are comfortable with. Consider:

The images in the card.

The pictures vary based on the artist and the designer There are cards which show the cards clearly, others with intricate symbols and images as well as ones which are basic in their designs and designs.

The creator and your feelings.

It is important to consider not the name (so to speak) rather, the intention of the person who made the cards. Things like intentions aren't easy to determine however, this is where your personal feelings play a role. It is important to pick one that is natural to you. Simply, go with your gut and choose a deck that feels like it speaks to you and is comfortable to feel.

If you're considering getting an astrological reading or are doing one on your own, it's normal to face the difficulty in understanding the information being provided to you. Tarot cards offer information on things you've asked them about or about a broad topic. The issue is that we're accustomed to either yes or no answers as humans operate. Sometimes, we can be lazy and would prefer someone other than us to make difficult choices for us.

The responses provided by a tarot deck more of a suggestion to listen to your thoughts, then take advantage of it to make a choice. If you are able to spend time delving into each card and the overall meaning, continue to think about their possible meanings, and you'll probably come across some helpful suggestions.

You should also know the significance of the cards as a whole. Let's consider the card that says "fool" and depicts a person falling off the edge of a high cliff. It could be a signification for any of different things. As you consider it, you may recall meeting a drunk friend who was about to enter his car and drive around in his condition. You arrive and insist that you drive. This could mean that the person walks away from the scene to ensure he'll arrive safely. These connections increase your understanding and improve your understanding of the cards.

People's reaction

If you decide to try an entirely new method of practice, people who are close to you, or perhaps people who aren't, may give their opinion or judgement. In the case of Tarot cards, they have strong opinions on it due to the widespread belief that it's a sin. This is an example of the fair and honest payment for the bad actions of people. If a person who is bad employs a hammer to harm people and cause harm, do you blame the hammer's manufacturer? It's the same with tarot decks. Tarot cards are a tool and the method used to make use of it is not on the tarot's own deck or the person who made this particular deck.

But, there's the possibility that many people won't comprehend or don't be able to comprehend. How can you continue to do something that people are constantly accusing you of? The answer is simple. Keep in mind that you are doing this to benefit yourself, not them. You are the only one involved and in the process and engaged, not them. The person who is playing the deck and reading is you not them. You're not harming them or causing harm, and they're not in any way involved. They should not care or worry about what you do during your personal time. So, you shouldn't.

Learning to master your sixth sense

When someone is looking to learn to read tarot cards, there is always a question whether I am able to do it? Do I have the right qualifications to do this? The answer to both questions is yes!

Anyone can read or the reading. There aren't any requirements. One of the main reasons for this kind of question is the myth that states that Tarot readers must be psychic. Being psychic is only a sign that the person is more in tune and has a greater understanding about their sixth sense. The sixth sense functions very similar to intuition. it gives you small bits of information or sense things as you're doing or about to perform something. Every person is blessed with it. It's just a matter of learning to pay attention and be able to comprehend the information being presented. It's all about practice so don't stress. In time, you'll gain a sixth sense and could be known as psychic.

The future is predicted by predicting the future

Do you believe this? No.

The Tarot cannot forecast or predict the future. The issue is that it uses the word predict. For the majority of people, it is a feeling of a certain end to it, akin to destiny. If someone tells you that the bride will get married at age thirty-five, she'll feel that there's no other choice, there is no alternative. It's inevitability. It is exactly what the Tarot isn't about. Consider it more of an encyclopedia of wisdom. An online resource to obtain details from, and serve as a reference, or a guide for consultation.

If you ask"Should I get married to that person?', the Tarot provides information regarding the issue. As for the intentions of the person's you, how it affects you, what you think concerning the matter, as well as aspects similar to that. In the deck, there might be some indications that this could be a mistake but that doesn't suggest that you shouldn't get married to the person, it simply indicates that, as it is at this point there are some concerns. Maybe if you had a more open dialogue or if the two of you changed slightly, or if you were able to see the other differently it could be that the issue would end up being resolved and then all would be fine.

Other general subjects are an additional aspect to watch out for. Let's say a girl wants to learn about her life with her partner as well as her family's future and discovered that she'll get married to the man she's always wanted to marry in ten yearstime, and then in another ten years they'll have three children. For interpreting this information, keep in mind to look over the fine print in contracts, not only the most important parts. The lady in question may refuse to marry every guy who is who is waiting to marry the one that the Tarot 'predicted' she would marry. Perhaps she doesn't desire that many kids, but accept it as something due to occur. However, that's not what the story says not at all.

Marriage in ten years implies that you might meet your perfect partner in the market one day, then become acquaintances for 3 years, go on dates for three moreyears, break the ice over a period of time, reunite back together, be married for four years and then file for divorce. As with having three kids in ten years , it doesn't say the presence of a husband or not. It could mean that you'll get an average of one child in three or more years. Or twins, and the third or triplets.

There are many things that can occur in that period of time, and it is best to keep it in your mind, but continue with your daily routine. The words spoken in a wedding ceremony aren't absolute and you have the option of choosing your own destiny. The woman could choose to be married prior to 10 years and she and her husband would like to have just one child. It is important to think about this for a few minutes, contemplating about the various things that each card might indicate. Don't take the information you receive immediately and swiftly. Keep your eyes open.

Chapter 14: Sample Reading

While doing an Tarot reading, it is important to be aware of these things:

Do not be a slave to inhibitions

Don't make assumptions.

Don't allow negativity to cloud your judgement

- Make sure that you're at peace before sitting down to read

To read a tarot card, there will be an issue you'd like to be able to answer. Check out the following example.

Seekers Question

This Seeker in this case is Inga. Inga's main concern was her relationship with her partner. The question she had was what was the reason why she couldn't have a long-lasting relationship with a man she liked. She was also curious about what the future would hold for her. Her astrological signification is Pisces.

Reader's Response

The reader utilized a contemporary Tarot deck and laid down the cards inside the Celtic cross spread, as described in Chapter 2.

These cards were drawn during the process of reading. They were numbered according to the order they were arranged.

High Priestess High

The Magician

10 of Cups: The 10 of Cups

"The Queen of Wands

The Devil

The Eight of Wands

2 of Cups. 2 of Cups

Wheel of Fortune

Judgment

The Knight of Swords

Each of the cards was described , and the significance was determined based on the person who sought them out. The significance for the card was determined by analyzing the characteristics and characteristics of the sought-after. Based on the reading , it was decided that self-analysis and contemplation could be effective to the person seeking. The counselor advised her to not be in a new relationship due to the pain of the one before. It also offered suggestions about how she should dress to match the circumstances.

It was determined that she needed to examine herself and find out what hindered her from realizing her dreams. The reason for this could be worry or the attitude of her. She was asked to get to know her self better, but not to be a victim of anything that was happening in the years. Only after you have a clear understanding of your self, can you come up with solutions.

She was instructed to remain vigilant and be patient. If she is prepared, she will be prepared to be in a situation where it is likely that an opportunity will strike.

Chapter 15: Full Completion of The Minor Arcana

A Tarot deck contains an overall count of 78 cards. It is known that 22 of the cards fall within the Major Arcana, which leaves the remaining 56 cards which comprise the Minor Arcana. The 56 cards of those of the Minor Arcana are further divided into four distinct groups each of which has four cards. The four groups are tied with one element and all of them are referred to as suits.

In each suit, there are 10 cards assigned a number starting with the ace and ending with the number ten. after that, there are four court cards, similar to what those you'd see in your common card deck. The cards with numbers reflect the scenarios that individuals confront in their lives, while the cards that represent the court show the persona or connect to individuals that are part of the life of the person seeking.

The suit is explained in this manner:

The Suit of Cups

This suit is closely related to the water element. The cards that are featured in a spread of this suit are a representation of one's mood, what's going on in their relationships, and what is the deepest of emotions. The emotions that are depicted go beyond what one can be feeling about themselves. These feelings also encompass the emotions that people feel with regard to others.

If you are presented with any of the cards listed, you are not trying to determine your logic-based conclusions in a particular situation instead, it will reveal what's going on inside your heart as well as the way that you typically react to specific situations.

But, when the card is seen in its reverse position, it indicates to the inability to control emotions and a situation in which your expectations are not having any base in reality. It could indicate that, within you is something you're trying to hide that's keeping you from being able to express your feelings.

Because these cards are comparable to the ones you'd see in a normal deck, they could be used in conjunction with an ordinary deck to serve the purpose of reading. It would be in the Suit of Hearts in such deck.

It's the Suit of Pentacles

This suit is in direct relation to the element Earth. Earth generally signifies stability, but in this case the cards focus on the realm of material and financial possessions since they provide the financial resources of one's and the things they actually own. Everything that is material is included in this suit, and they are also a reflection of what is taking place in the work or profession.

When it appears to be in an upright position in a reading, it focuses on what's going on in your financial, health and work areas and the way you've changed or altered your outer environment to create the conditions you're experiencing in these areas of your life. This, in turn, is connected with how you think about your self.

If this card is seen in reverse the card could be a sign of negative characteristics, such as levels of greed in which one puts too much emphasis on goods that are material and neglects to take good care of one's body or health. This could be a sign of an issue where financial situation is not properly controlled, or someone is so busy that other aspects of their lives suffer due to.

In a standard deck of cards, this suit could be symbolized as The Suit of Diamonds.

Suit of Swords: The Suit of Swords

This suit is closely related to the element Air. It is able to reflect the rational thought process as well as the actual thoughts and levels of thinking. This also influences the amount of power one might have. With this power, cards in this suit may reveal how people use their own force and how much ambition they have and also their ability to manage conflicts. When dealing with conflict, it is possible to decide to take actions that have an outcome that is positive, however, sometimes it could result in negative in the other case.

The suit examines what's happening in the mind, so it can draw conclusions from the basis of mental awareness. They have multiple edges It is therefore necessary to find the right balance, or else one could play with good as easily with evil.

While this suit conveys the positive aspects of this suit however, should it seem to be inverted once presented, it exposes the very strong negative aspects also. This includes hatred and the creation of enemies. If one reads the card one could be able to discern anger, and an inability to feel compassion for the person or circumstance. In the worst-case scenario the card can identify possible abuse by the person either verbally or mentally.

It is the strongest among the suits. In a normal card deck the swords could be symbolized by The Suit of Spades.

The Suit of Wands

This suit is linked to the element Fire. This is the fourth among the 4 suits and is a symbol of the individual's spirituality as well as the things that give them ideas and motivation. It also indicates how an individual's energy might flow. If these cards are revealed in the reading, they reveal that one is determined to achieve a specific objective, and has the power and determination to ensure that they achieve this objective. The cards will reveal what's happening inside you in the deepest part and tap to your subconscious at a deeper level. This means that your character will be revealed through the deck of wands.

In a story they discuss the various factors that keep one engaged throughout the day. This can include working or staying inside. They consider the various methods that they can be able to take action in their time and interests.

If these cards are displayed on the reverse side, they carry a negative significance, pointing to the situation in which one engages in reckless behavior, or when there isn't any need for one's existence. They could also be revealing the circumstances of those who have lost interest in life, and it seems to be as if it has no value.

If a person wants to perform a reading with the standard deck of playing cards, the suit will be symbolized in Suit of Clubs. Suit of Clubs.

Chapter 16: Spreads, or How to Place The Cards To Give A More Actual Reading

Once you've got some basic understanding of the primary meanings of the cards, it is time to continue to study how you can use them to help you read. There are many ways how you can accomplish this and many skilled readers come up with in time various methods to come up with an answer to a particular query. The most essential kind of spread is the Celtic Cross. It is the most popular spread, and if you can master its rules, you'll be able to make the transition into the more complex spreads.

The Celtic Cross

Elements:

The Circle. This particular section (the one that has six cards) is representative of feminine traits. It is comprised of two circles which are called The major (the two cards that are located in mid-line) along with the larger (the two lines which surround that minor cross). The middle card are the most intense concerns during the reading. The cards of the horizontal line (from left to right) symbolize your progression from the past to the present, and the cards on the vertical line (from the bottom to the top) symbolize the difference between the unconscious and your conscious.

The Staff. Its area (the horizontal line that connects the cards) is not directly related to the question, however it provides you with a general perspective of where you are in the world. It's also referred to in the "side comment" section.

So you have various possible positions for the cards. The next paragraphs will provide some insight into the various ways that you can interpret a specific card based on its place it is within the cross. I've written all the number on every of the cards, to allow you to understand the meaning behind each position.

Position 1. Position 1. The card that is that is in Position 1 is the central aspect of the issue (you or the issue affecting you). It is your personal perspective in the scenario and will reveal the primary (dominant) aspect to be aware of.

Position 2. Like the position it's located (crossing the issue) This card is the second element that can affect your circumstances. It is typically unpredictable and is in opposition to your primary sources of knowledge. It could also indicate the reason you aren't able to solve an issue.

3. The most common understanding of the card that is in this position is "that that's below you". So this could be the source of your problems and the cause of the most trouble. It is usually in your subconscious, which is the result of your secret desires, which you have not fulfilled.

Position 4. In the situation of the past This card will reveal what is hindering you and preventing you from fully living into the next time. It doesn't need to be negative However, it's an issue which has been resolved and shouldn't be given the same significance to you in the present.

Position 5. This card will reveal what you believe in the present moment to be the truth (your current desires, preferences or worries). It is what your subconscious imagines as the most desirable alternative for the coming years.

Position 6. The cards in this position will provide information about an aspect that could be the focus of your focus in the near future. It may be something that you started in the past and failed to full-time attention, or must be taken seriously today.

Position 7. The card you see in this spot will show the way that, even at the subconscious level, you view yourself and your place within the world. This can include your own personal strengths as well as your self-confidence level as well as your limitations, fears and your ideal self.

Position 8. The components of the card in this situation represent the way people perceive you at this moment, or as tradition suggests, "that which surrounds you". This could be a general impression of the world about the way you conduct yourself or the opinion of others about how you have handled a particular issue.

Position 9. This card can provide an insight into the aspects you ought to have thought about, however, due to a reason, you did not admit their importance to the solution you're looking for. It could also be a sign of your unresolved fear and the source of your anxiety. Whatever the case it is important to be addressed as well since it may be the root of your issue.

Position 10. The card will provide you with a an overview of the result, and the manner it will be resolved at the final. It could also include the effects the actions you take on people around you and the whole world around you.

Chapter 17: Read For Yourself And Others

Tarot Reading Tarot for yourself

Reading a tarot card to yourself can be a spiritual approach to gain insights into your life's successes as well as its difficulties. Although it's a device which can be utilized anytime you're in desire, it is in a unique location and in a particular plane. It's not your typical vacuum cleaner or broom you keep in the closet, or similar to the favorite screwdriver that is inside your toolkit. To gain access to the mysterious knowledge of the Tarot it is necessary to spend just a moment and let your subconscious know that it's the right time to connect. This can be accomplished by following these steps:

Create a space of your own for your readings. If you don't have enough space within your home, get a separate reading mat which you can place in a tranquil area whenever you're ready for the Tarot reading.

The subconscious mind of children is and attracted to sensory stimulation, so we engage in activities such as burning incense and light candles, or play music that soothes us to to get our subconscious and conscious minds in sync and prepared to transmit information back and back and forth.

Although we would like to tap into the subconscious, it is important to begin with clearing the conscious. You can accomplish this by engaging in a deep breathing practice for a couple of minutes before we begin to shuffle the cards.

In the right Frame of Mind

Being receptive to the world is much easier than you believe. First, you must learn to separate your feelings prior to going to read. You can unpack them afterwards--certainly after you've had time to go over the results of the reading. Everyone experiences emotions when we look at the cards in the Tarot reading. Sometimes these emotions are elation or joy, as well as hope and at other times, they're fearful, sadness or even disappointment. The outcomes of reading a Tarot reading may be quite a challenge to digest.

Expectations and feelings prior to the reading will certainly impact how the results of your card This is the reason we make sure to keep an open and uncluttered mind when we enter.

And Again...and And Again (Avoid the temptation of drawing more cards)

The most frequent mistake made by experienced and new Tarot reader is to second-guess their own cards and drawing what they consider"a "qualifier" cards. If you are unsure of your qualifications, take a look at the cards you initially chose to draw. Examine their meanings. If you discover ones that aren't understood (the Moon, for instance which is known for its in obscurity) Consider it an indication that the answer just aren't there in the near future. You could try a different examination in a month or a week to determine if additional details are available.

If we continue to draw cards following a reading, and second-guess ourselves, it's permitting doubt to cloud our work. Doubt could undermine and our subconscious mind's connection with the world. Do not be a doubter at any cost.

Three Time's the Charm--Second-Guessing Your First Reading

It is a given that reading a second time shortly after the first one is going to take the "qualifier" impulse of the card to the limit. It isn't easy being unsure of all the details, but if you accept the urge to read that can turn into obsession. Note down what you read take a moment to thought for a minute or two, then put the notes away and go on with your life! Don't let the tools control you. We make tools that we can use to improve our lives and make life more efficient.

Alternative meanings (How to Rely on Your Intuition Before you decide on a Standard Definition)

After we've gotten through the process of not thinking about our abilities, we're about to face an actual test. When you've used the Tarot cards for several months, you might make a decision to draw a card, and then experience what we refer to as"a "wow" moment. This is when your intuitive sense immediately gets an unambiguous and precise message. Note it down. If it isn't in line with the card's original meaning do not fret. Whatever you need to do to get the information out to your mind, your subconscious will try to implement it. Don't dismiss the information just because it's not standard.

Reading to help others

If others in your life discover that you've started playing Tarot cards, then you may be receiving many calls for readings. This is a great opportunity to gain knowledge and become accustomed to the cards. Don't be frightened you have to be an expert reader to offer an interpretation and don't feel ashamed of needing to refer to the book. But, at the same time you can tell if reading for others is not your thing Don't be compelled to accept it. Simply let them know that it's a hobby for you however, you're willing to steer them to the right path should they decide to pursue the pastime for themselves.

Forget Everything You Think You Know (About the other person)

If you choose to read to another person, you're going need to spend some time to calm your mind and organize the space. Two people's energies may mix and leave imprints of spirit across the room. Think about "smudging" the area by using sage, palo-santo wood, or rosemary prior to you begin. It is also possible to take turns in smudging one another: just use the wood or burning herb and rotate it in counterclockwise circles prior to the other person, from head to foot.

Before you begin before you begin, it's possible to listen to another person explain what's happening in their lives and the reason they'd like to get to get a Tarot reading. If so, listen to the other person's story with an objective and objective ear. Be aware that you aren't supposed to incorporate your emotions in a reading. It's a channel at this point, bringing data from all over the world to another person in a manner that is hopefully helpful to them.

If you suspect that they've been experiencing financial hardship, for instance don't seek evidence of this in their cards. Do you remember those five-of-pentacles deck which shows homeless people in a church sat outside? This card in an individual's reading could mean nothing whatsoever to do with money. It could actually be reflecting on how depressed the person is regardless of the offerings of friends and family who are around them.

Being open to new possibilities is the most beneficial way to approach your client's Tarot reading.

Chapter 18: Step-by-Step Instructions for the most important readings

This chapter will show you how you'll be able to move from the theory to the practice. After having been familiar with the theory of tarot and tarot readings, you have the basics of the most commonly used readings The private reading (a personal reading of yourself and about others) as well as outside reading (when you're looking for the specifics of the other person) as well as generally reading (when you're not particularly interested in a particular issue but simply wish to learn more about your overall position within the global community).

The Personal Reading

This is likely to be the kind of reading you'll likely to use the most. It is a great option to get a specific response that you'd like to hear or for a routine reading when you need to know what you can anticipate from the next (or the present) day. This means that you can conduct this reading before you go to bed the night before you awake and get ready for the new day. You could study for yourself anytime when a specific circumstance arises all of a sudden and you feel you need to gain relevant understanding of what you need to do.

The most crucial thing about the reading that is personal is that it should be, as the title suggests personal. It should be about the person you are reading for and about. The other person cannot be implied, either directly or in indirect ways. You can, however, examine, for instance the manner in which you must behave towards the person who is near to you however the person of interest should remain your personal. Another factor that may be just as beneficial to you as it has been to me, is to keep journals. In writing about your progress over a longer time, you'll be able observe the cards you have chosen more frequently and assess if these aspects you chose really reflect your character and your daily life and if there's any adjustments you could consider making.

The External Reading

If the earlier type of reading has to be focused on your personal needs and preferences some kind of reading, we also require something that can provide us with information about other things that aren't directly linked to us. The readings may be related to individuals, the general future or a specific occasion, animal, or even the whole world. The concept is that the ultimate conclusion of the question is based on the scope of your inquiry is: for questions that concern groups, or for instance the future of our planet the answer is very ambiguous.

This is the reason you must choose a particular area of interest, that is the center of interest. The question you note down, and which you'll be able to repeat (aloud as well as in your head) as you move the cards. While I have stressed that, in order to interpret this reading, you should get your subject out of the issue It is important to realize that, in interpreting the results, you may be surprised to discover that certain aspects could be yours too. These kinds of situations are common when you attempt to find out something about someone near to you.

The General Reading

Another strategy that may be beneficial in the near future is to conduct a general reading and asking your tarot card to help you navigate your evolution in the near future. It is common to require this type of reading in times of stress or overwhelmed by a cause that we are unable to comprehend. So, by conducting an overall investigation, you can discover the root of - perhaps in the unconscious level your stress. However, you may perform the reading without any particular interest. In this scenario this should be done at least once a month and, in the best case just prior to major events in your life (in order to maintain it at a different level that your usual everyday readings).

To do this, there's no requirement for a specific problem to be reduced to a specific question. This is the reason you can take the next step on the next list and replace it with more careful focus on your own thoughts, and the things you want to know more about. It is possible to express your trust in the ability of the cards and trust your intuition. Additionally, you can perform several general readings when you are looking to narrow the subject matter of your you are interested in. For instance, one time you might consider your relationship with someone and then your health and then on and on.

9 Steps You Must to Follow to be Successful in Reading

1. Set things up and gather all the things needed to complete your reading. Before beginning the actual act of reading, you'll need to be aware of everything else that could cause interruption. That is clearing

your mind of any distractions that could hinder your ability to focus: feed your pet and give your children something to do to keep them entertained and take care of your essential daily chores, shut off your mobile and other things like that. Prepare the cards and head to your designated spot.

2. Get into the state of mind. Like I mentioned in the earlier chapter (go back in case you need the information to read them again) An appropriate mindset is required to be able to read. Relax, and reflect on the issue which is currently causing you stress. Once you're ready, grab a piece and note down the proper answer to your query.

3. You can ask the questions. Once you've attained the required concentration level, grab the cards you hold and contemplate your issue. Then, you can ask the question in front of your peers as if the person who would be able to give you with the answer was right before you.

4. You can also shake the deck. While you are still contemplating the issue and the overall background of your issue then begin shuffling the cards. Keep doing this for as long as you'd like and in the way you feel most comfortable.

5. The cards should be cut. Once you're done shuffling, place the whole deck before you. Split them into three smaller piles beginning with one card inside you're drawn to. Put these back into the same pile. Keep in mind that the cards have to remain in their original position.

6. Distribute the cards into the shape you would like (The Celtic Cross in our case). Make sure to carefully make the pattern by placing the cards on you. These cards must be placed in a straight position.

7. Analyze the cards. Try to recall the significance of each card and in the same way consider the place where they're put. Pick those elements that are the most suitable for your specific circumstance. Be objective and objective. Record the most

important factors, if you believe it will assist you to make a better understanding.

8. Combine the results to determine the general meaning. Check to see if can connect the distinctive characteristics of each card so that you can create a sort of storyline from the past to the present, or from unconscious to the conscious, for instance. Try to write down the complete understanding, in order to get the answer you need in a single sentence for your inquiry.

9. What's next? After putting the cards into order, you need to consider the actual reason behind the question. How can the answer benefit you? What can you do to rectify your mistakes from the past, and also respect or practice the concepts you just learned about? Prior to returning to your regular routine, be sure to discover an opportunity to put these new information into the context of your daily routine.

Chapter 19: Pentacles

Pentacles are a different term for diamonds that are used in the original playing deck . they also symbolize the element Earth while their decks focus on the physical body or possessions.

Ace of Pentacles: Upright: someone who will be able to create a new financial situation, wealth, and an example of wealth. A reversed person is someone who's not prepared mentally or plans properly, or missed the chance to be lucky.

Two of Pentacles - Upright one who has equality in their life, excellent time management, can change their life anytime, and knows what their primary concern should be. In reverse: someone who is in financial chaos, and extremely chaotic and confused.

Three of Pentacles: Upright: Someone who has experienced the first time of success through cooperation, collaboration and knowledge. In reverse: someone who doesn't recognize the skills of others and isn't able to cooperate.

Four of Pentacles: Upright: discipline, strength control, ownership, and moderate. In reverse: overly seeks, is mostly focused on physical objects, and worries about self-protection.

Five of Pentacles: Upright: unsure of self-esteem, isolated, worried financial burden

Or losing money. In reverse, someone is getting over financial or spiritual losses.

Six of Pentacles: Upright: Someone who is generous an altruistic, generous wealthy and successful. In the reverse: greedy, thinks only about their own personal wealth and what they can take from people and owes money to other people.

Seven of Pentacles: Upright: diligence, awareness and someone who is able to earn the benefits of money, gain and assets. In reverse: does not have an eye for the long term and has only a few accomplishments or praises.

Eight of Pentacles Upright: Someone who is about to begin their training and will feel an attraction or awe at their task. The reverse is one who is a perfectionist who is always looking for perfection but doesn't have the desire to be successful and has trouble concentrating.

Nine of Pentacles: Upright: someone who is unpretentious lavish and indulgent and is able to look after their needs. The reversed meaning is someone who's suffered or is likely to suffer an economic mishap and who will spend too much on their work.

Ten of Pentacles: In the open: possessions, money, acquired through the death of someone and organization, withdrawal from work, and the family. In reverse: experiencing financial loss, failure and loneliness.

Page of Pentacles: Upright: the possibility of a an employment opportunity. The reverse is No advancement or gain due to short-term focus.

Knight of Pentacles Upright: habit, resistance to change, efficacy or specific. Reversed:

Someone who is feeling uneasy disinterested, bored and uninterested.

Queen of Pentacles Upright: Someone who is ordinary, compassionate real, honest, in fact, and secure. In reverse: someone who is unstable in the workplace and with family obligations.

King of Pentacles Upright: Someone who is secure, under command, strong, ready and generous. The reverse is brutal, overbearing and controlling

Conclusion

This is the guideline to look up if you're beginning to learn. It gives you all the details you need to know when you are learning about the Tarot beginning with the history of the deck to the cards that are in the deck. It helps you comprehend what the meaning is behind the cards that are in the deck. It is recommended to utilize the spreads listed inside the guidebook! Helps you learn quickly.

It is important to remember that you're still a beginner and you may be prone to mistakes in the beginning. It's okay! As a youngster, learning how to ride a bicycle you would fall over and over. However, you always came back to your feet, and then began to go on again. Be aware of this when learning how in reading, and understanding Tarot cards. If you're not sure about your abilities, try giving yourself a reading prior to deciding to give someone else. In the beginning, you should make use of Three Card spread.

Three Card spread since that is the easiest to master and you will not commit mistakes. Once you have mastered the art of it, you can use the two spreads that are mentioned in Chapter 2.

The various cards have been explained in detail, and can assist you understand the process. There are 78 cards it may take you some time to grasp the meaning of each. With practice and time you'll understand their meanings and be able to talk about them without needing to reference this book. The main concept is to be able to tell a story in a spontaneous event that helps your clients get a great reading experience and feel satisfied.

Be careful not to reveal a grave reading, as it could lead people to be worried. Make sure to keep it straightforward and simple , and always finish the reading in a positive way. They've come to you because they believe in you , and you must meet your commitment to give them a trustworthy and authentic reading.

www.ingramcontent.com/pod-product-compliance
Lightning Source LLC
Chambersburg PA
CBHW071842080526
44589CB00012B/1088